YOUR
GERMAN SHEPHERD
PUPPY

YOUR
GERMAN SHEPHERD
PUPPY

Ernest H. Hart

illustrated by the author

I would like to thank all those wonderful and co-operative people who breed and own German Shepherds and who supplied me with the photos for this book. Among them may I mention; Charles Griffin, Jane G. Bennett, Valerie Wilson, John S. Neff, Robert J. Andrews, Mrs. Joan Sic, Betty J. Irwin, Josef Wassermann, Ernie Wilck, Nikolaus Seeman, Fran-Jo Kennels, Hermann Nierman, Fred and Tina Becker, Max Lipp, Erich Beckman, Clare and Elli Matlin, Werner Freund, John and Barbara Ellis, and the German S.V. Special thanks to my son, Allan H. Hart, B.V.Sc., for his invaluable aid in the chapter on health and medicine.

to Katie

and her Shepherd shadow, Blanka.

Title page:

The personification of German Shepherd puppy appeal, Bee Jay's Tonka of Robline at six weeks. sire: Ch. Britmere's Timothy of Lahngold; dam: Bee Jay's Sugar. Owned by Bob and Lynn Andrews.

ISBN 0-86622-039-9

Distributed in the UNITED STATES by T.F.H. Publications, Inc., 211 West Sylvania Avenue, Neptune City, NJ 07753; in CANADA by H & L Pet Supplies Inc., 27 Kingston Crescent, Kitchener, Ontario N2B 2T6; Rolf C. Hagen Ltd., 3225 Sartelon Street, Montreal 382 Quebec; in ENGLAND by T.F.H. Publications Limited, 4 Kier Park, Ascot, Berkshire SL5 7DS; in AUSTRALIA AND THE SOUTH PACIFIC by T.F.H. (Australia) Pty. Ltd., Box 149, Brookvale 2100 N.S.W., Australia; in NEW ZEALAND by Ross Haines & Son, Ltd., 18 Monmouth Street, Grey Lynn, Auckland 2 New Zealand; in SINGAPORE AND MALAYSIA by MPH Distributors (S) Pte., Ltd., 601 Sims Drive, # 03/07/21, Singapore 1438; in the PHILIPPINES by Bio-Research, 5 Lippay Street, San Lorenzo Village, Makati Rizal; in SOUTH AFRICA by Multipet Pty. Ltd., 30 Turners Avenue, Durban 4001. Published by T.F.H. Publications Inc. Manufactured in the United States of America by T.F.H. Publications, Inc.

CONTENTS

FOREWORD

There is much that goes into the fashioning and the nurturing of the young of any species, and this is particularly true of the dog. No one knows better than the breeder the trials and tribulations, the hopes, dreams and anxieties that accompany every litter from the moment the stud is selected and the bitch comes into heat, until the animals that are conceived from the subsequent breeding reach adolescence and maturity.

To watch a puppy grow, especially a Shepherd puppy, to care for and train it, to keep it well and vigorous and completely adjusted to its environment as it reaches toward adulthood, is a thrilling experience for both the breeder and the owner, if they are separate people. The Shepherd puppy is not just another young dog; it is, indeed, an important part of the family that owns it, influencing greatly that segment of life, those years, when it participates in the activities of the family group.

To help you make the most of that time when the Shepherd puppy shares with you a given interval, to aid you in extracting the last measure of pleasure from ownership of the youngster, and to ease for you the sometimes trying period of puppyhood and adolescence is the purpose of this book.

I would like to take this opportunity to thank all those good people and earnest Shepherd fanciers who sent me the many fine photographs of their Shepherds, in all stages of growth, that grace these pages and give it added pictorial value. Particularly must I extend my most sincere thanks to Clare T. Matlin who gathered these photos for me to publish in this book.

Ernest H. Hart

Chapter 1.

THE SHEPHERD PUPPY BEFORE BIRTH

The mystery of mammalian birth is an intriguing part of the complete dog breeding concept. One moment there is nothing but an impossibly obese bitch in a whelping box, apprehensively aware of the stirring of new life within, and attended by an anxious owner. The next moment, with the onslaught of labor pains and peristaltic movement, there are two animals in the whelping box, mother and canine child. The phenomenon of nativity has taken place and will continue at regular intervals, you hope, until genesis is complete and a fine and healthy litter of pups feed greedily at nature's milk bar.

But long before the puppies come into wriggling being they must be fed well to insure absolute and maximum health and vitality when they materialize from the mother's warm, protective womb into the harsh reality of life. The vehicle through which we accomplish this purpose is, of course, the mother bitch. She must be fed well for her own maintenance and for the normal development of the young in utero, particularly during the last thirty days of the gestation period.

The bitch must be in good health when she is bred. If she is not nature will generally take a hand and delay the coming of the heat period. She should be mature, not bred

Young, awkward as a teenager, full of mischief yet eager
to please and gain your approbation, this sixteen weeks
old male obeys the "Sit!" command.
Owned by James Vogel.

at her first heat, and a sound, healthy, typical specimen of the breed. A sample of her stool should have been brought to your veterinarian for a fecal examination shortly before her mating cycle began and, if there was any evidence of internal parasites she should have been wormed, with a repeat dosage to follow within a week or ten days to eradicate any worms that may have hatched from worm eggs that were not eliminated. The bitch should *not* be wormed any later than a week after she has been bred. Any drug that can kill internal worms can also harm the tiny, forming embryos within the pregnant female.

Fenja v. Piastendamm, SchH. II, sire: Falk v. Bubenlachring; dam: Ortrud v. Piastendamm. A German bitch of lovely breed bitch type.

The mother-to-be should have had sufficient exercise so that she will not lose her muscular "tone" and overall strength and vitality. And, of the utmost importance, she must have been fed well and intelligently. By *intelligently* I mean that she should not be stuffed with supplements, the means some frantic breeders use in an effort to insure the whelping of healthy pups. Feed the bitch the same healthful, well-balanced diet you have been giving her and feed her enough, but don't stuff her until she becomes fat. A fat bitch is never an easy whelper. A vitamin and mineral supplement should be incorporated into the food but used

Della v. Devrienthof, SchH. I, HGH. Sire: Volker v. Zollgrenzschutz-Haus, SchH. III; dam: Antje v. Ahnenschloss, SchH. III. Twice German herding Siegerin and a top "V" bitch in conformation, Della was imported and owned by the author.

moderately. Many breeders philosophize that if a little bit is beneficial a lot will be that much more advantageous. The result of such irrational thinking is a heavy handed application of supplement in the feeding pan to the detriment of the healthy, nourishing, and extremely necessary bulk food of the regular balanced diet.

Every bit of food you give the bitch is nutritionally aiding in the fetal development within her. She must be provided with

Caret v. Elfenhain, SchH. I. sire: Alf v. Nordfelsen (Sieger); dam: Anka v. Elfenhain. One of Germany's great producing bitches, Caret was mother of the "C", "D", "G" and "H" litters vom Sixtberg. Owned by Max Lipp.

enough milk to produce calcium, meat for phosphorus and iron, and all the other essential vitamins and minerals in her high protein diet. By incorporating fresh liver in her food two or three times a week a month before she is due to whelp, you will keep her from being constipated and aid in the coming, necessary production of milk for the litter. As the embryos develop the bitch's appetite will increase to keep up with the demand made upon her by the growing whelps. In the last two weeks of her pregnancy it is desirable to provide her with a hearty breakfast as well as her usual dinner, and a drink of milk between meals will also help feed and nourish the hungry, soon-to-be-born babies. The most important factor in puppy survival is the level of nutrition during gestation and the post-parturient period. Linked to this element of puppy survival is the genetic formula of the whelp which mirrors its affliction to heredity and congenital diseases, abnormalities and anomalies.

The puppies develop in the horns of the uterus, not in the *"tubes"* (Fallopian tubes), as is commonly thought. As

Number 8 on the diagram indicates developing embryos in the pregnant bitch. The other numbered parts of the female reproductive system are: 1. Vulva 2. Anus 3. Rectum 4. Uterus 5. Kidney 6. Ovary 7. Ribs 9. Vagina.

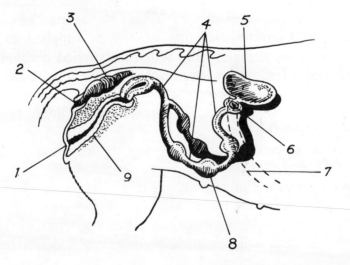

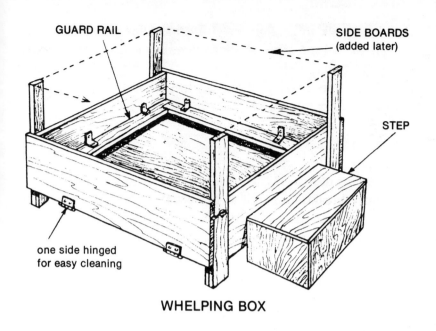

GUARD RAIL

SIDE BOARDS
(added later)

STEP

one side hinged
for easy cleaning

WHELPING BOX

they develop, the uteri horns lengthen and the walls expand to accommodate the rapid growth of the embryos. This embryonic growth of the puppies is a process of division of cells to form additional new cells, and at each cell division of the fertilized female eggs each of the chromosomes also divide. These chromosomes are the gene packages, the inherited characteristics that have been supplied to the puppy by his sire and dam. When the myriad divisions of cells and chromosomes have reached completion the forming of a living entity is accomplished and birth becomes a fact. Then, in the whelping box, we see before us a living, squealing, Shepherd puppy.

Death at birth, and unthrifty puppies that either die or fail to mature into strong, healthy animals, is due to several causes. *Infection* in any area of the female's reproductive system is one of the main causes of puppy deaths, before or after birth. *Close inbreeding* can cause a genetic linkage of lethal or semi-lethal faults that have been dormant in the

germplasm for generations only to become obvious by affecting the embryonic puppies. *Improper feeding* or lack of sufficient and nutritious food is another factor that will cause puppies to be born dead or weak. Late, pernicious *dosing* for worms can bring harm to the unborn whelps, and breeding the bitch too often without a rest (particularly if her environment is not all it should be) can also bring disaster in its wake. *Eclampsia*, sometimes called milk fever, is a metabolic disturbance prevalent in pregnant bitches whose diet lacks in calcium and phosphorus. If she had been getting a good, balanced diet and plenty of milk, this condition is avoided. *Mastitis*, an udder infection, is a common cause of puppy deaths. It is generally mistaken by the uninformed for "*acid milk*", a condition which does not exist in dogs because the bitch's milk is naturally acid. The infection cuts off part of the milk supply and the whelps either die of infection or from starvation due to the lack of sufficient milk.

When labor begins pressure from within forces the puppies, one by one, toward the pelvis. Make sure that you have removed all long hair from around the udders to make them easily accessible to the pups when they arrive. Wash the udders in warm water and a bland soap, then rinse all soap off thoroughly and dry so that they will be clean for the coming nursing. The whelping box should have been made familiar to the bitch at least a week before she was due to whelp. A piece of oilcloth or rubber sheeting can be used as a base flooring for the whelping box to make it easy to wash and clean. On top of this can be laid newspaper, which will be removed after the whelping is completed. The main bedding for the bitch and her pups should be either hay straw or torn up paper. Hay makes excellent bedding because it retains its fresh smell and imparts a pleasant odor to both the dam and her puppies. The size of the whelping box should be roughly 4 foot by 4 foot for a bitch the size of a German Shepherd. The whelping box should be fitted with a rail all around on four sides. The rail should be a few inches above whatever material is used for bedding. If young puppies are pushed by the dam's body against the side of the whelping box, the rail will prevent the mother's body from crushing them.

Each puppy is born in a fetal envelope called the *amniotic sac* which the bitch will tear open. If she waits too long to do this then the human attendant must break the sac open around the pup's face so it will not suffocate. Often the sac will rupture during birth and the puppy will be born leaving

Moni v. Passargetal, SchH. I. sire: Kondor v. Piastendamm; dam: Heidi v. Passargetal. This fine German bitch was in whelp. She was bred to produce fine puppies.

the sac still within its mother. The navel cord is connected through the sac to the placenta which generally accompanies the puppy at birth. If it is retained and the bitch chews off the cord that attaches it to the puppy (a completely normal and necessary act), the female will normally discharge from her uterus the lining to which the placentae were attached along with the placentae through which, during pregnancy, the young were fed.

Some bitches whelp rapidly, others don't. But if several hours pass between the whelping of one puppy and the next it is best to call your veterinarian for expert advice. Don't worry if the pups are born head first or feet first; either way is normal.

Since this is a book about puppies and not about bitches and their breeding and whelping, I will delve no further into these aspects. The important thing to remember is that whatever you do, or whatever happens to the bitch, from the moment she is bred and the embryonic life within her caused by the breeding begins to form, also affects the

A beautiful trophy table at a large California show.

Seven times Select, Ch. Tucker Hill's Angelique, C.D., R.O.M. sire: Holland Sieger Gauss v. Stauderpark, SchH. II; dam: Jodi of Tucker Hill. A magnificent bitch who produced many great offspring. Handled by Cappy Pottle; owned by Pottle and Birch.

puppies that will eventually be the end result of that breeding. So bring her to the mating in good physical shape, not exhausted from constantly producing puppies at every heat; feed her well with a nourishing, balanced diet before and during pregnancy; give her adequate exercise and supply her with a happy and familiar environment. Then, if all goes well, you will have a fine litter of healthy pups from your bitch which should be a credit to both your breeding acumen and your knowledge of animal husbandry. And, another and important consideration, you will show a nice profit from the sale of the pups to happy and satisfied customers.

Family portrait. Mom, Dad, and two of the kids. The sire, on the left, is Condor vom Sixtberg, SchH. II, A.D., the dam, Della vom Devrienthof, SchH. I, HGH, both animals imported and owned by the author.

Chapter 2.

THE SHEPHERD PUPPY BORN

The time of waiting is past. We have planned the breeding carefully, selected the right stud dog and have anxiously awaited, with great expectations (apologies to Dickens), through approximately 60 trying days and nights for the blessed event which has at last taken place.

Now, though the puppies are being born and the whelping is proceeding with nice regularity, you cannot yet relax. As each pup is born, and after the mother has been given ample time to lick and clean and fuss with the tiny whelp, you must put it on the mother's udders, first squeezing a little milk to the surface from the chosen nipple. Then by holding the puppy's head and forcing its mouth against the teat you will spark instinct in the little creature and it will begin to suck and push against the udders with its front feet.

All young that are obviously not normal should be culled at birth. A pail of water near the whelping box is the easiest vehicle for this chore. Do *not* cull abnormal young immediately if they are the first to be born. Wait until the bitch is occupied with newly born normal pups, and is about to again give birth before you stealthily extract the abnormal pup from the nest.

Usually the pups first born are the largest, particularly if the litter is a large one. This is due to the fact that the pups growing in the furthest part of the uteri horns sometimes get less nourishment than the others. But, once born and given equal opportunity to feast at nature's banquet, the smaller pups generally make a hasty size recovery and equal their formerly larger litter mates.

19

If the bitch whelps six or less pups and all seem normal and healthy no further culling is required. If she has a particularly large litter it does not pay, in the long run, to allow her to attempt to raise all the whelps without help. Let her keep six or seven of the best and cull the rest.

You will find that, by culling large litters down to reasonable size, the pups retained will grow better and be healthier and possessed of more vitality than if you allow the entire, large litter to live.

Parasites become serious threats between ten days of age and weaning time. Add this to navel ills, pneumonia and enteritis, and combine with poor environmental conditions and, in their entirety, they contribute largely to morbidity and mortality in very young puppies.

Quiet puppies are healthy ones. Constant crying and squirming of the pups is a danger signal and a check should be made to see what ails them. Sometimes the trouble is parasitic infestation, navel infection, or possibly coccidiosis. It may be that the bitch is not providing enough milk and they are hungry, or perhaps they are cold. This latter cause,

The lovely bitch, Fidelco's Asta, owned by the author. Sire: Frack v.d. Burg Arkenstede; dam: Ulla v. Schweigerts-Eck. She was nursing a litter of eight males by Condor vom Sixtberg.

Ch. Sarego's Quality. Sire: Brando v. Aichtal; dam: Zola z.d. Sieben Faulen. A lovely bitch owned by Charles Griffin. Photo taken at three years.

not generally taken into sober consideration by many breeders, can be a major reason for the weakening and death of puppies in cold climates during the winter season. Frequently a tiny, blind whelp will manage to squirm away from its dam and litter mates and, unless its mother rescues it and brings it back, it can become fatally chilled before the breeder sees and helps it. The chill, combined with the pup's inability to nurse while not in contact with the mother, weakens it to the extent that it can no longer fight for position at the canine dining table provided by its dam and it goes down hill rapidly.

Puppies whelped in places where heat is lacking must be given survival aid. I advocate soft straw or hay bedding for the whelping box for this reason. If the bedding is deep enough the mother (sometimes with your aid) will form a saucer in the middle of the straw or hay in which the puppies stay with little chance of moving away at this early age. The dam curls around this indentation giving the whelps easy access to her milk-filled udders. The pups are always close to each other therefore each lending its body warmth to the other.

Actual heat can be provided through the medium of any kind of coal stove or gas or electric heater. Or an electric bulb (preferably infra-red) can be rigged up with an extension and an inexpensive green, almost flat shade, to hang over the whelping box.

A new electric heating pad developed by the Goodyear Company offers a very definite solution to the problem of lack of heat in the kennel, pen or whelping box. These vinyl 24 by 33 inch pads, called Pliotherm Kennel Heaters, are easily installed, easily cleaned, and probably the best answer to keeping puppies in the nest warm. Every effort must be made to maintain an ambient temperature of between 86 and 92 degrees Fahrenheit in the whelping box.

There is nothing much you can do for the pups in the first few days except to examine the navels to see that no infection has set in (the cord left after the dam has chewed it rapidly dries up and drops off), and to remove the dew claws, if any, from the hind legs.

The dew claws should be removed on the second day after birth with the aid of a pair of ordinary manicuring scissors. A small pip of blood will appear at the site of the removed dew claw and the pup will emit a wee cry. As soon as these extra toes are removed return the pup to its mother. She will lick the tiny wound and keep it clean so that it will heal rapidly.

If, for one reason or another, the mother cannot feed the puppies I do not recommend that you attempt to do the job yourself. If, under these circumstances, it is possible to find a foster mother for the pups your troubles are over. Most lactating bitches will readily take to puppies other than their own if the new babies are first prepared by spreading some of the foster mother's milk over their tiny bodies. The foster mother will lick them clean and welcome them to her nest. If your bitch's litter is too large and you wish to keep and raise all the puppies, again the foster mother plan is the best.

If you cannot find a foster bitch and decide to hand raise the litter you must remember that the most important requirement of newborn pups is proper food. Puppies are all belly and instinct and little more. They must be fed well and frequently. What formula can we feed these mites that will most closely approach the combined ingredients that nature provides them from their mother's breasts? Not pure cow's milk, as we can see at a glance by comparing the composition of the two liquids.

	Fat	Protein	Carbohydrate	Ash	Water
DOG	11.2	5.7	3.1	1.3	78.7
COW	4.0	3.8	4.1	0.7	86.2

But, since bovine is the only milk available, we must use it as a base and modify it to more closely approach bitch's milk. To do so we must specifically increase the fat and protein content. This can be accomplished by adding melted sweet butter to the milk. A little cream and meat blood will bring up the protein content, the cream also adding some fat. The addition of a beaten egg yolk will also modify in the desired direction. Goat's milk has been proved valuable in puppy feeding, as has the inclusion of evaporated milk in the formula.

Another, and perhaps even better formula, utilizes Pelargon, a Nestle's spray-dried, acidified and homogenized modified milk product. As a substitute for Pelargon, if it is not available, use any other fortified, spray-dried baby milk product. To one ounce of the modified milk product add one ounce of fresh cream. Pour six ounces of water by volume into this mixture and blend with electric mixer or egg beater until smooth. Large amounts can be mixed employing the same basic proportions and kept refrigerated until used.

Yet a third way to feed just-born puppies is to purchase a prepared modified milk, especially manufactured for orphan puppies, which is commercially available and very much worth while.

Whichever formula you use must be fed five to six times a day and, when fed, must be warmed to body heat. Many puppies refuse to accept a formula that has not been warmed to just the right temperature. Do *not* add lime water, glucose or dextrose to the formula, for by doing so you are modifying in the wrong direction. Avoid using an eye dropper for feeding unless you put a drop at a time on the puppy's tongue and make sure he swallows it, a tedious business and one that is too long drawn out to be sensible when feeding a litter. Inhaling milk fed from a dropper can cause pneumonia and death. It is best to use a bottle and nipple. A normal size baby's bottle and nipple for pups the size of Shepherds.

The puppies should be fed the following amounts of formula.

PUPPY WEIGHT	AMOUNT OF FORMULA
12 oz.	1 oz.
1 lb.	$1\frac{1}{2}$ oz.
2 lbs.	2 oz.
3 lbs.	$2\frac{3}{4}$ oz.

Note : *The above amounts are to be provided at each feeding and are approximate, since puppy capacity varies as does human.*

The easiest way to feed orphan puppies is through the use of a tube which is pushed down, through the mouth and into the stomach. Use a number 10 French tube and a large syringe. Use Esbilac or any good bitch milk replacer. Feed 3 to 4 times daily, 20 cc. to 25 cc. per one pound of puppy. Be sure that the milk is kept at a 90° heat while feeding; 1 cc. of for-

A pair of nice puppies by Ch. Harry v. Donaukai, SchH. III (sire of double German Sieger, Volker v. Zollgrenschutz-Haus) and out of Ch. Jola of Popular Creek, bred and owned by John S. Neff.

mula equals 1 calorie and it is necessary to feed 60 calories per pound of dog a day. This is called "gavage" feeding and is also quite helpful for saving debilitated puppies that are too weak to suckle. Gavage feeding can be utilized for the first ten days, but after that you must shift to the nursing bottle feeding to satisfy the puppies' sucking needs or they might begin to suck their own flesh and cause sores. Incidentally, the puppies' eyelids are sealed until ten days after birth, and their ears are not operational until they are thirteen days of age.

Today the Fading Puppy Syndrome or Puppy Septicemia, is well known to most breeders. During the first week various bacterial agents are the cause. After the first ten days, herpesvirus takes its toll up until the puppies are about three weeks of age. Puppies in the nest become weak, cry constantly, their skin wrinkles and dehydration occurs. The tiny stomachs of the whelps are evidently painful to the touch and, as breeders so often describe it, they seem to "fade away, one by one," and die in from 12 to 18 hours. The temperature of the stricken pup is generally, and surprisingly, normal. Protect the pups from stress conditions which help to initiate this syndrome, such as chills and an unsanitary environment.

To treat puppies that show even the faintest signs of being affected by Fading Puppy Syndrome, follow the ensuing program:

1. Raise temperature in whelping box to a minimum of 80°F.

2. Feed Esbilac or a replacer milk formula if there is any question as to the quality or quantity of the mother's milk.

3. Initiate supplementary feedings of raw liver juice every 8 hours.

4. Give antibiotic (pediatric) drops (especially chloromycetin or tetrocyclin) every 8 hours.

5. 2 to 3 cc. gamma globulin (concentrated serum) is of great help in combating this killer of pups.

Give the puppies this treatment for from 4 to 5 days. The recovery rate is excellent for puppies that survive the first 48 hours, especially if the disease is of bacterial origin.

If you encounter this syndrome in your whelping box and lose the first pup it is advisable to have your veterinarian perform an autopsy on the puppy and have cultures made

A two-and-a-half weeks old litter of four males and two bitches, by Kurt v. Bid Scono x Zsa Zsa of Twin Lance, bred by Mrs. Joan C. Sic.

from any pathological organs, especially the liver, lungs and intestines, so that specific antibiotic medication can be employed. The cost of such a procedure is but a fraction of the value of one good puppy and may be instrumental in saving the lives of the rest of the litter.

Many of these infections are transferred interuterine; therefore a culture of uterine discharges, just before whelping or, preferably, at the beginning of the next heat period, may identify the causative organism and, with proper treatment of your bitch, fading puppies may be eliminated and even improvement in fertility achieved.

Peak milk production of the bitch occurs two to three weeks after whelping. Very definite neurological and physiological changes can be found in the puppies at this time. Daily human contact should be initiated during this period and a supplemental hand feeding program practiced daily to facilitate development of the coming canine adult behavior and the social integration between canine and human.

Let us hope that you will not have to hand feed your litter and that the bitch is healthy and has plenty of milk. If so it is best not to handle the pups much or allow them too many visitors. Both mother and babies need peace and quiet. Don't allow the bitch to spend all her time with the whelps. She will need exercise and a rest from her brood several times a day. If all is well and the bitch taking good care of her young, as she should, you will not need to be bothered with them for about $2\frac{1}{2}$ weeks.

Chapter 3.

WEANING THE SHEPHERD PUPPY

Under normal circumstances it is best to begin supplementary feeding when the puppies are from $2\frac{1}{2}$ to 3 weeks old. Watch the whelps carefully when they nurse to be sure that they are getting enough milk from the mother to fill their bellies. If they hang onto a nipple, sucking enthusiastically and fall asleep, replete and satisfied, you can be sure that the bitch is providing them with maximum nourishment. But if they move frantically from one teat to another, sucking and searching, and their stomachs do *not* fill up, you will know that the bitch is no longer supplying them with enough milk for their growth and well-being.

It is known that at least 43 essential nutrients must be supplied in the canine diet to create an optimum cellular environment for complete metabolism. Included in this group of essentials are an energy source, fatty acids, amino acids, vitamins, inorganic minerals, oxygen and water.

Often when a bitch has a small litter of one or two pups her milk will begin to disappear much earlier than if she had a full litter to feed. If the mother has been bred too often without a rest her milk may go before it should. Even if the mother has enough milk to continue to feed the whelps substantially she will often engage in an instinctive

A beautiful portrait study of a lovely female. The feminine quality of this bitch is very evident. She is Hexe's Bella of Highland Hills, by Stoutheart Ray-Mor's Adjent x Hexe of Highland Hills, owned and bred by Clare T. Matlin.

The three weeks old "X" litter of Twin Lance, by Ch. Waldenmarks Ilko x Insa v. Gellnhausen, bred by Charles Griffin. The sides of the whelping pen will soon have to be made higher to keep the puppies in.

and natural action when the litter is from $2\frac{1}{2}$ to 3 weeks old. She will regurgitate her stomach contents of partially digested food for the puppies to eat, thus serving notice, in her own way, that weaning time has arrived. If you have begun supplementary feeding in time, this action by the bitch will seldom occur.

To begin the process of weaning use any one of the formulas advocated in the previous chapter for orphan puppies. Pour some of this liquid mixture into a shallow pan after heating it to body temperature. Use only enough of the milk mix to cover the bottom of the pan. With one hand hold the pan just below the puppy's chin and, with the other hand, grasp him gently by the head just behind the ears and, without exerting force, dip his chin and lips into the pan. Release his head immediately and he will lick his lips and like the taste of the liquid he finds there. Speak to him quietly and in an encouraging tone as you repeat the process. Sometimes a puppy will begin to lap the pan milk after the first contact; sometimes it will be necessary to repeat the performance several times. You might find it necessary to hold the pup's chin in the pan until he begins to lap.

Be very careful not to pour too much of the milk mixture into the pan, or to push the puppy's head too far into the liquid. It is imperative that the pup's nose is held clear of the new food so that he will not breathe in the liquid or clog his nasal passages with the milk. If this occurs the whelp becomes frightened, eyes the pan with distrust, and the process of weaning becomes more drawn out and exasperating.

Repeat the process with each puppy until all have begun to lap of their own free will. It will be necessary to hold the pan at chin level for the pups during the first few feedings. But once they become expert at eating, or lapping,

The same "X" litter of Twin Lance pictured on the facing page, but at four weeks of age and gathered around the milk pan. Note the difference in growth just one week will make in young puppies.

Charles Griffin with Insa v. Gellnhausen, dam of the "X" litter, when she was ten months of age. She was by Condor v. Hohenstamm x Isa v. Stuhrigau.

from the pan it can be put down on the floor. Of course they will crowd and step in it and smear themselves and their litter mates with the pan's contents. But they will also become more proficient in the process of eating from a pan which is the ultimate goal.

Feed the mixture twice a day for the first two days. By the end of that time the act of pan feeding will have become a conditioned routine. It is then time to add fat and some solids to their diet. They cannot yet chew so any solids added should break down into tiny pieces to form a heavy-cream consistency when fed.

Puppies grow best on *milk, meat, fat,* and *cereal* diets. Growth is attained through proteins mainly, but proteins

From the "X" litter of Twin Lance bred by Charles Griffin, this is Xingu of Twin Lance at eleven months.

differ, so that puppies fed on vegetable protein diets will not grow and thrive as well as those fed animal proteins. Vitamins E and K (*found in alfalfa meal*) are essential to the pup's well being and must appear in adequate amounts in the diet. Remember that 70 percent of the youngster's energy is derived from fat intake, so supply this food element generously in the ration. In experiments, puppies on fat-free diets developed deficiency symptoms characterized by anemia, weight loss, dull coats, loss of vitality, and finally death. Fat alone could not cure the advanced manifestation of the condition, indicating that some metabolic process

At only eight weeks of age note the striking secondary sex characteristics exhibited by these pups by Condor v. Sixtberg, x Della v. Devrienthof. The male is on the right, female on left.

was disturbed when complete fat removal in the diet was resorted to. But feeding butterfat plus folacin resulted in dramatic cures. Fat also acts as a vehicle for carrying the vitamins A, D, K, E. It slows digestion so that the animal gets all the nourishment possible from its food, and helps in many other ways to keep a puppy, or fully grown dog, healthy and vigorous. To give your puppy all the virtues inherent in fat he should have 20 to 30% incorporated in his diet.

Practically every breeder you meet has his own weaning and after-weaning diet. The basic necessary element in any diet is balance, and a properly balanced food must be one that produces growth, health and vitality. There are fine commercial puppy foods on the market, in grain form, to which one need only add milk and fat. Or one can purchase grain human baby food such as Pablum, Ceravin, or those advertised as "high protein" and "fortified" children's foods. These, too, must be modified to fit the dietary needs of canine babies.

The author uses a mixture of rolled oats and rolled wheat as the basic cereal. To this, while it is cooking, is added 1 cup of vitamin fortified corn meal; dried, powdered eggs; rendered fat (beef fat, lard, butter, Crisco, chicken, etc.); ground beef; a little salt; and powdered milk. After this mixture has been cooked and cooled, a small amount of a vitamin and mineral supplement powder is added, thoroughly mixed in and the thick food spooned into quart jars and refrigerated.

To make it ready for immediate use, the necessary amount is spooned out into the food pan; ground, raw, fatty meat is

At five weeks of age, Hexe's Arry of Highland Hills, by Ray-Mor's Adjent x Hexe of Highland Hills, bred by Clare T. Matlin.

Note the bone and quality displayed by this seven weeks old male puppy, sired by Condor v. Sixtberg, SchH. II, A.D. and bred by the author.

added (ground beef hearts, tongue, tripe, and a small percentage of liver), to increase the amount fed by about 25 percent, and evaporated milk mixed with water. The milk and water mixture is heated and when added to the solid mix heats it all to the proper temperature. When mixed the food has the consistency of very heavy cream. This consistency is gradually changed to a thicker, more viscous mix of porridge-like texture by the time the pups are 4 weeks old.

A word of warning here. Overfeeding (hyperphagia) studies made with German Shepherd puppies indicated that overfeeding resulted in higher evidence of hip dysplasia developed at an earlier age. It was more severe in Shepherds having a more rapid growth rate as the result of an increased caloric intake as compared to dogs on restricted feeding programs. The Germans do not overfeed their puppies, as we in America have a tendency to do. As an end result they seem to have less dysplasia than we do. Incidentally, elbow dysplasia is seldom found in German Shepherds.

35

When the litter is 5 weeks old a good finely ground grain dog or puppy food is gradually introduced to the basic diet. And by the time the pups have become $6\frac{1}{2}$ to 8 weeks old, the original formula has been eliminated and they are fed the grain food with fat and the raw meat, with milk and meat broths to give the proper consistency.

A valuable adjunct to the puppy's diet is a good feeding oil (such as *Dietol*) or a fish liver concentrate oil. A drop in the lip pocket of the pup the day after birth and each day for a week, to be followed by 2 drops, then 4 drops until weaning, when the oil can be added to the food fed. Be very careful and do not overdo the feeding of any supplementary dietary oils or you may provoke the very kind (in appearance) of bone trouble (rickets) you are trying to prevent by their use.

Two feedings of the basic diet and two of warm milk fortified with a little fat should be given every day. When fully weaned three feedings of the basic diet and two of milk should be given. From three months to six months only three meals a day need be given.

Writing here of feeding reminds the author of a litter of pups he raised in Spain, on the Andalusian coast near Malaga. There was no dog food to be had and all the ingredients had to be bought raw and prepared from scratch. Wheat and lentils had to be soaked overnight to soften them enough for use. Meat was highly priced and scarce so I purchased spleen, lungs, tripe and dried blood (the latter cooked and fashioned into blocks). The dried blood was wonderful for the pups. For both mother and pups I found it necessary to cook huge pots of the ingredients listed above to which I added vegetables, rice, olive oil and beef suet. And to which our maid, Carmina, would stealthily add a clove of garlic. Cod liver oil and powdered calcium phosphates could be purchased in a "*farmacia*".

Incidentally, the veterinarians in that section of the world know little about dogs and have no serums for the dread viral or bacterial diseases. It was necessary for me to send a hurry cry for help to my veterinarian son, Allan, who immediately dispatched a "care" package with all that was necessary to keep the pups healthy and free from disease and worm infestation.

The bitch who whelped the litter was a fine daughter of *Volker v. Zollgrenzschutz-Haus* whom my wife and I had seen and admired at the Sieger show in Germany where we had stopped on our way to Spain. We negotiated for and bought her and had her shipped to us in Spain after she had been bred to a good stud, *Bob v. Reidkanal*. The puppies she whelped we sold in Spain. They were big, healthy, heavy boned, and understood commands in English, German and Spanish.

During the time we are occupied with weaning and feeding the pups we must not forget that there are other chores to be done. The puppies' nails should be kept clipped down with a manicure scissors so that they will not scratch the eyes of their litter mates in play. Their eyes will have opened when they were from a week to 12 days old (according to the bitch's time of ovulation), and will be blue until they later change to their true brown color.

When the pups are $3\frac{1}{2}$ weeks old a fecal check should be made by your veterinarian to ascertain if they have worms (*and most puppies do*), and what kind. If they are infested with worms, worm them immediately. If the worms have made them unthrifty do not attempt to build them up before ridding them of the parasitic infestation. After the worms are gone the whelps will speedily return to normal health and plumpness.

Also, before the pups are completely weaned, and preferably while they are still feeding at the dam's breasts, it is wise to consult with your veterinarian about a planned series of protective inoculations and vaccinations. A new distemper serum (human measles serum) is available which can be given to puppies at a very early age, even while still nursing. This serum, given by intramuscular inoculation, is not affected by the natural immunity the puppies have while imbibing their mother's milk, an immunity which makes the regular immunization vaccines negative.

This new vaccine is effective until the puppy has gone beyond all the important phases of early growth and when he is approximately six months old he can be given the regular immunization vaccine for distemper. Incidentally, the worms most puppies are heir to are the common round worms. *Piperazine* is less toxic than most worm medicines

Seven times Select, the very lovely Ch. Tucker Hill's Angelique ROM, C.D.; sire: Holland Sieger Gaus v. Stauderpark; dam: Jodi of Tucker Hill.

A group of handsome young puppies in Van Cleve Kennels owned by Dr. Carmelo Battaglia.

and the puppy can be fed normally, so that this class of drugs can be recommended for round worms, whose larvae in the bloodstream of the mother bitch often cross the placenta to infect the pup before birth.

You will find further information about your puppy's health and feeding in later chapters.

Most people worry about whether their pup is gaining enough. One way to tell is by observing their overall condition, their plumpness and vitality. Another way is by weighing the pups and keeping track of their gains. From six weeks of age to full growth a satisfactory average gain per week, for a fast growing and healthy Shepherd pup, is about 3 to 4 pounds.

Remember also to introduce your pup to water as a beverage at an early age. At first they don't seem to see it or know what it is, but they soon learn to lap it up just as they do their milk and milk-mixed food, and it is a valuable, mineral-rich adjunct to their diet.

Early, but very gentle, human handling of German Shepherd puppies is essential to later character development. The more attention paid the litter by the breeder the quicker any small ills can be recognized and treated so that the growth of the pups is not retarded.

Chapter 4.

FEEDING THE SHEPHERD PUPPY

In a previous chapter (3) we learned quite a bit about feeding puppies during the process of weaning. But there is still a good deal to know about the foods and feeding methods you must employ to bring your puppy to healthy, robust maturity.

There are certain factors that will retard puppy growth that we must be cognizant of if we would defeat disaster. Some pups that have been doing very well suddenly stop their precipitous rate of growth or lose their appetites which causes their growth rate to slow down almost to a halt.

When this occurs we must immediately find the cause and correct it. The growth of puppies is an explosive thing that must reach completion in a comparatively short space of time. Children have eighteen or more years to grow to full maturity, or until the skeletal structure reaches maximum growth. German Shepherd puppies show a skeletal freeze at about 11 or 12 months of age.

If anything happens to the puppy in those early months to slow or stop its growth and if whatever the cause may be continues for any length of time, the puppy will never mature to his full genetic worth.

Worms are the first thought when the pup or puppies begin to do poorly. Sometimes worms can be detected in the stool, sometimes not, unless put under a microscope where the eggs can be seen and identified. Another cause of unthriftiness can be *disease*. If either of these is the reason for the pup's decline your veterinarian should be consulted at once and either the disease that is the causative agent identified and treated, or the worms, if they are the culprits, identified and eradicated by specific drugs or expellents.

Puppies will generally pick up and swallow anything that they find, and this can result in bad damage to internal organs and/or death if the foreign body they swallow was one of the various poisons found in any household. This tendency to chew and swallow things other than food can also result in surgery to remove stones, wood, or other foreign bodies that have lodged in the intestines.

Lice can also cause loss of appetite and finally death if not eliminated. If enough of these tiny leeches infest a puppy they will cause anemia along with loss of appetite, and death as the end result. Examine your puppies carefully if they go off their food or fail to gain, to make certain that the common dog louse is not the cause. If it is, de-lousing powder is the immediate answer to your problem with added vitamins, proteins and some liver, raw or cooked, added to the diet for about a week until the whelps are back to normal.

A change of diet can also put your pup off his feed with an accompanying weight loss. It is always better therefore

Arcella, at three months. Owned by Valerie Wilson, the puppy is by Jorrens Daggonet x Haidee of Ridge Hill.

to attempt to keep the diet unchanged as much as possible with any alterations or additives gradually introduced so there will be no abrupt difference in taste or texture of the food. Frequently (as a matter of fact, almost always), a pup bought from a breeder and brought to a strange home by the new owner, goes off his feed and quits gaining as he should. This is most often due to the fact that a change in diet is made by the new owner. It is best, therefore, for the purchaser of a puppy to duplicate the diet to which the puppy is accustomed with as much fidelity as is possible. Another reason for loss of appetite in this case is because the pup misses its litter mates and familiar environment.

Sometimes puppies are born with intussusceptions, which means that an area of the intestines has telescoped. Surgery is the only answer to this problem, for the pups are unable to digest their food and are also in pain.

One inescapable reason for weight loss in puppies is *teething*. Inevitably the time comes when your puppy will lose his baby teeth and replace them with an adult set. This will occur at about 15 weeks of age, and for approximately six weeks it will continue until the puppy has all his new teeth. During this period the gums of the canine youngster are swollen and sore and the act of eating becomes a painful experience. As a result, for about a week the pup will eat very little and his weight gain will slow almost to a stop. At the end of this first week of teething the pup has generally become accustomed to sore gums, ignores them and eats with the same animal gusto as he did previously.

If for any other reason than those listed above, your pup or puppies do not seem to be thrifty and do not exhibit the healthy appetites and gains in weight that you think they should, consult

Charles Griffin with Sarego's Quality at seven weeks of age, the puppy that matured into a champion and a fine producer.

your veterinarian and let him, a professional, cope with your problem. Beware of parvovirus. This killer strikes down puppies quickly and without pity. (More about parvo in the chapter that deals with immunization and vaccination.)

From puppyhood to full growth, it is a mistake at any time to drastically change the animal's diet or eating habits. These habits you shape in the pup when he is young and constantly hungry should be adhered to throughout the animal's lifetime. Change turns dogs into finicky eaters, and finicky eaters are an abomination. Dogs do not need variety in their diets as do humans. Your dog can smell separately all the various ingredients that are mixed into his food pan,

Head study of "V1" Condor v. Zollgrenzschutz-Haus a Sieger Volker son, owned by the author.

so that each meal, though the same as the last, is nevertheless a delicious variety of intriguing odors and tastes, a diverse and delectable banquet fit for a king . . . and what Shepherd is not a king in his own home?

To realistically approach the problem of feeding for maximum health, strength, and vitality in maturity, we must weigh the canine's needs against the food substances available to us.

The Shepherd is a *carnivore*, a flesh eater. His teeth are not made for grinding, they are chiefly fashioned for tearing and severing. This has led to the erroneous conclusion that

Grand Victrix Ch. Covy's Rosemary of Tucker Hill ROM; sire: G.V. Ch. Lakeside's Harrigan ROM, dam: Ch. Tucker Hill's Angelique ROM. A sensational career for a fantastic bitch. Handled here by Gloria Birch, owned by C. Pottle and Gloria Birch, Roberts judging and Bob Hamilton, then Chairman of the G.S.D.C.A. board of governors.

the dog must be fed mostly on a muscle meat diet in order to prosper, and this idea came, of course, from observation of the feeding habits of the wild canines, the wolves, dingoes, jackals and foxes.

But, these feral, carnivorous cousins of the Shepherd consume the entire body of their prey, not just the muscle meat alone. First these wild hunters lap the victim's blood, then they tear open the stomach pouch and consume the stomach and its contents, composed of predigested vegetable matter (*the main prey of these wild cousins of your dog being the hoofed herbiverous animals, and also small mammals and birds*). They then feast on the liver, heart, kidneys, lungs, spleen, and fat-encrusted intestines. They crush and consume bones and marrow, fatty meat, connective tissue, and finally the muscle meat. They slake their thirst at the nearest stream after their meal and, through the agency of one hoofed animal (deer, sheep, calf, colt, goat, kid, etc.) have absorbed minerals and assorted proteins, fats, fatty acids and carbohydrates, vitamins, and roughage for proper laxation. From the sun that shone on them as they ate, and from the water they drank afterward, they absorbed supplementary vitamins and minerals. To supply the same essentials to our dogs in a form which you can easily purchase is the answer to their dietary needs.

For health, vigor, and normal growth puppies and adult dogs must be fed all the food essentials, and these necessary ingredients can be found on the shelves of your local grocery store. There you can buy all the natural sources of the dietary necessities in the list that follows.

1. PROTEIN: *meat, dairy products, eggs, soybeans.*

2. FAT: *butter, cream, lard, oils, milk, cream cheese, suet, fatty meat.*

3. CARBOHYDRATES: *cereals, vegetables, honey, syrups.*

4. VITAMIN A: *greens, peas, beans, broccoli, asparagus, eggs, milk.*

5. VITAMIN D: *fish liver oils, eggs, fortified milk, some fish.*

6. THIAMINE: *vegetables, whole grains, eggs, milk, yeast, muscle and organ meats.*

7. RIBOFLAVIN: *milk, liver, egg yolk, yeast, wheat germ, beef, chicken.*

8. NIACIN: *milk, lean meats, liver, yeast.*

9. ASCORBIC ACID: *tomatoes, citrus fruits (not necessary for dogs).*

10. IRON, CALCIUM AND PHOSPHORUS: *milk and products, egg, blood, liver, oatmeal, bone marrow, vegetables.*

The first three listed essentials complement each other and compose the basic nutritional needs. *Proteins* build new body tissues and are composed of amino acids, which differ in combination with the different proteins. All living cells are composed of protein molecules so proteins are essentially the basic elements of life itself. *Carbohydrates* furnish the fuel for growth and energy, and *fat* produces heat which becomes energy and enables the dog to store energy against emergency. *Vitamins and minerals*, in general, act as regulators of cell activity. All other vitamins, the *B-complex, E and K*, are contained in a well rounded diet, as well as the so-called *Vitamin F*, which is actually the unsaturated fatty acids.

Milk, perhaps the most complete of all natural foods, lacks in iron content. But puppies, unless plagued by hookworms or lice, are born with enough iron stored away to last for the several weeks of milk diet they must endure until just past weaning time when they get their first solid food. The meat in that food will supply them with all the iron they need. Puppies when very young need vitamins E and K. They manufacture their own E as they do vitamin C, and the K they get in their mother's milk and also in any balanced diet fed after weaning.

WINNERS BITCH

Lucas

48

Ch. Covy's Rosita of Tucker Hill, ROM; sire: Covy-Tucker Hill's Zinfandel, ROM, dam: Ch. Covy's Felita of Tucker Hill, ROM. The author awarding winners bitch to this lovely young bitch. G. Birch handling.

All the proteins, vitamins and minerals are important to the puppy's health. But any of the balanced diets recommended in this book, or meat, milk, fat, a sprinkling of vitamin and mineral supplement, with a good manufactured dog food as a base, will supply all of these nutritional elements the pup needs.

Some of the trace minerals may become of greater importance in the future than we ever dreamed they would be. Just recently *Zinc,* important to growth, but thought to only be necessary in so small an amount in the mammalian body to produce results that its presence is recorded as a "trace", has been found in the research laboratory (*by a fortunate accident*) to have another, and very important, function. It almost miraculously aids in the growth of tissue, so that the healing of wounds, through the agency of added zinc intake, becomes a far quicker process than ever before thought possible. Zinc aids also in the production of a luxuriant coat.

Canned, or *pudding foods,* are good. But remember that they already contain the liquids necessary to mix the ingredients. They are especially good to feed when traveling with your dog, or when at a dog show. Practically all canned dog foods contain 78% moisture, so you are feeding mostly water and a minimum of real food staples.

Canned meat, chicken, lamb, etc., displayed on your grocer's shelf for dogs are very good to add to the basic milk, cereal, fat, mix. *Biscuits* are good to clean the puppy's teeth, massage his gums, and give him some nourishment and food value, but a good deal of the vitamin and mineral content of a biscuit has been destroyed by baking, so they cannot be considered a balanced diet. Some of the *kibbled biscuits* have this same disadvantage. But the *grain* foods and *pellet* type foods are very fine, balanced dog foods. Add to a good grain food some fat (20% to 30%), milk, meat and meat broths, with a small sprinkling of a powdered vitamin and mineral supplement, and you can be sure that you are feeding your dog well. Some animals prefer something more to chew than a grain food provides and for them the pellet

Ultra of Twin Lance at fourteen months, also a daughter of Sarego's Quality, but by Bernd v. Kallengarten, a very good sire. Below is Yum-Yum of Twin Lance at seven months, by Zando of Twin Lance (a son of Sarego's Quality) x Insa v. Gellnhausen. Both bred by Charles Griffin. Note how compact and well-put-together the seven months old puppy appears while Ultra (dark in color like her sire) exhibits the typical adolescent ranginess of her fourteen months.

Condor v. Stoerstrudel, SchH. I, the import and Grand Victor 1963, proved to be a good producer in America. His untimely death deprived the fancy of many fine youngsters like the puppies shown below. He was owned by Thomas L. Bennett and Fred Becker, Jr.

type food (*grain food to which a binding agent has been added*) is the answer.

The author prefers to add vitamins and minerals to the diet in as natural a form as possible. To this end I mix Brewer's yeast, alfalfa leaf meal, green ground edible bone meal, salt, and a bit of bicarbonate of soda (the latter to neutralize stomach acidity). Instead of Brewer's yeast, irradiated yeast can be used. As already mentioned, commercially prepared vitamin and mineral supplements such as Vionate, Paltone, Pervinal, etc., are excellent.

Please heed this warning relative to the usage of supplements; do not overdo them! An overdose of most vitamins will be carried away in the bloodstream and not harm the individual. But there are some vitamins, or their vehicles, that can prove very harmful if given in too large a dose over

Tiny pups, like this one, need vitamin and mineral supplements, but in discreet quantities. This little fellow seems to have big ideas for the future as he eyes the tree trunk.

a period of time. Cod liver oil, used as a vehicle for vitamin D, if given in excess over a period of time, can cause toxicity and malformation of the bone similar in clinical aspect to the very disease (*rickets*) that it is used to prevent. A fish liver oil concentrate is much better to use.

Calcium and *phosphorus* in pure chemical form must be handled with care when used in the puppy's diet. Toxic conditions can be caused by an overabundance of this material in the bloodstream.

Water is one of the elementary dietary essentials. Considering the fact that the dog's body is approximately 70%

water it isn't difficult to understand the importance of this staple to the animal's well being.

Water is one of the major sources of necessary minerals, helps to regulate the dog's temperature, and prevents dehydration. It is also the least expensive part of the animal's diet, so supply it freely, particularly in warm weather. But, when you are housebreaking your puppy, only give water under supervision. A puppy who has water available will drink all day, and a puppy who drinks all day will piddle all day.

If you are feeding only one or two puppies or dogs, table scraps can be included in the diet. But be sure that for the most part, and day after day, the basic diet is used. This practice will prevent that bane of the dog owner's existence —a finicky eater.

The consistency of the food you feed young puppies must be soft and creamy. As they grow older the texture should thicken and take on greater body. At six months a wet, sloppy mixture is not relished by most dogs, so the consistency of the food should be denser and drier.

If, because of a change of diet or a liking for some specific food or table scrap not provided, your puppy refuses to eat, remove the food pan and do not offer it to him until the next feeding time. Be sure, of course, that the pup is healthy and is not refusing food because he is ill. He may refuse the second or even the third time offered the food pan. But hunger will eventually drive him to eat when it becomes acute enough and he realizes his hunger strike has done him no good.

Do not ever leave the food pan in front of a puppy who will not eat for more than 15 minutes. If he hasn't touched his food by then, remove the pan and offer it again at the next meal time. Remember that during these tender weeks you are aiding the puppy to form the food habits that will remain with him all his life, so shape them to your will and convenience, not his. He is also, through the food pan, being conditioned to obey you in other ways which will prove fruitful later during training.

Wash all pans and utensils used in the puppy's feeding immediately after usage. Each time you feed, the pan should be completely clean and never display dried particles of food along the edges left from the last meal. All food given the pup or puppies must be fresh and refrigerated if perishable. Make sure that nothing mixed in the food has turned sour since the last time used.

Following is a chart indicating the age of the puppy and the consistency of the food it should be fed.

AGE	FOOD
weaning; 2½ weeks (feed twice a day)	*liquid, orphan puppy formula (for 2 days)*
weaning (feed 3 times a day)	*Heavy creamy consistency. Add solids. 2 meals a day of mix, one of milk fortified.*
4 weeks	*Thicker, porridge consistency mix. 2 solid meals, 2 of milk.*
5 weeks	*Add grain puppy food to mix. 3 meals of mix, 2 of milk.*
6½ to 8 weeks	*Original mix eliminated. Feed grain puppy food, meat, fat, milk and meat broths. Milk meal.*
3 months to 8 months	*3 meals of mix. Eliminate milk meal. At 6 months begin to add adult dog food, kibbled or grain.*

Supplements can be added to the food mix at 3 or 4 weeks. Food should be served at blood heat until 3 months. After that make sure all food has had the chill removed and is served at room temperature. Water can be supplied after each meal from 4 weeks on. After housebreaking, water should be made available at all times. From 8 to 18 months, feed 2 hearty meals. Fully adult dogs usually require only one meal a day.

Vigorous, healthy Shepherd puppies at sixteen weeks of age. Their ears are coming erect nicely and the tan coloration will cover greater areas and become more evident as they mature.

Chapter 5.

REARING THE SHEPHERD PUPPY

The little mites that you have bred and brought into the world, or the tiny puppy that you have bought and brought home are, or is, completely dependent upon you for care.

Good husbandry pays off in dollars and cents, for clean, well-cared for puppies are generally healthy puppies free from the small ills that bring greater woes in their wake. Healthy puppies are, in turn, more saleable and at better prices, and need less expensive veterinarian care.

Puppies need exercise and sleep; a good deal of sleep as does any young mammal. They will, of course, begin to play with each other in the whelping box soon after their eyes are fully opened and they are able to move around with some assurance. But they need play in the fresh air as well. These outings relieve the monotony of the whelping box and its surroundings.

Select a warm, sunshiny day for their first introduction to the out-of-doors and provide them with a pen, so that they will not roam too far (if you do not have a kennel run for this purpose). This wire pen can be of heavy mesh chicken wire, about 3 feet high and with metal stakes at each corner. It should be set on grass to simulate the hay surface the puppy has been familiar with in his whelping box. This can be the beginning of housebreaking, for the puppy will prefer to eliminate on a familiar underfoot surface and will realize that such a surface is outside.

The puppy pen can be about 6 feet square for 1 or 2 Shepherd puppies. Remember that the Shepherd pup is of working stock and can be given this outdoor play time even though the weather is cold. If the sun is out and you bring him in before he begins to chill, such winter outdoor time will do him good.

Never take baby puppies in the streets or visiting. The only time the pup should leave the place where it was bred and born is when it is sold and brought to its new home. Too many elements of illness and contagion to which it has no resistance, can be encountered by the small pup removed from the environment to which it has adjusted.

Take the puppy out and put him in his pen for playtime, immediately after feeding. Generally a half to three quarters of an hour of playtime (particularly outdoors), will result in an hour to two hours sleep. Puppies need this sleep so they must not be disturbed. If they are young during the summertime when the sun is high and hot, provide shade for them in the play pen. This is easily accomplished by throwing a piece of canvas over the top of the pen to shut out the rays of the sun from at least half of the pen area.

While the puppies are young and ravenous with the hunger of all young, growing things, is the time to condition them to sharp sounds so they will not be sound-shy later. This can be done by making such sounds while they are eating. Actually, if you do a bit of hammering close to where the whelping box is when the pups are still nursing and haven't yet opened their eyes, they will become accustomed to sound, accepting it as a part of their environment. But, if you wait until later when they are pan feeding, keep the sounds fairly soft at first, then increase in volume and sharpness, so that the loud crack of a hammer striking wood, the top of a pail hitting the floor, the quick clapping of hands, or the firing of a gun close to them will have no effect and they will continue their frantic feeding as though they hadn't heard a thing.

Though this is the type of training indulged in by gun dog breeders, and we are not concerned here with gun or sporting

The bitch above is Panthre's Delight of Delilah, owned by the Fran-Jo Kennels and the dam of the two puppies on this page. At right is Krys of Fran-Jo, by Rikter v. Liebestraum, below, Vacca's Donna of Fran-Jo, by Lance of Fran-Jo. Note how the dam's nice type and sable color has been transmitted to the pups and the longer neck and hindquarter bones passed on by Lance.

dogs, it is nevertheless a necessity to accustom your pups to such noise so that they will not be sound shy. A German Shepherd must not be shy in any respect or he is not worthy to bear the breed name and the utilitarian significance of which it is indicative. Sound sureness in the breed is a *"must"* in Germany, and if you expect to work your dog in obedience or Schutzhund it is a necessity. It is, after all, merely an adjunct to good temperament.

Feeding utensils should always be kept clean. Heavy aluminum or light pressed steel feeding and watering pans are best, since they are easily cleaned and do not chip as do agate and porcelain. Feed the pup or pups regularly at the same place and at the same time. Establish a friendly and quiet atmosphere during feeding time and do not encourage the youngsters to play at this time. It is meal time and they must learn to apply themselves to the food pan without outside distraction.

Watch the puppies when they are eating. There are always the slow eaters or the less aggressive ones who get pushed aside and therefore fare less well at the feeding pan.

Ten weeks old puppies out of the good bitch, Bessie of Villa Sica, bred and owned by Mrs. Joan Sic.

Handsome, strong-boned and typically male, Hexe's Arry of Highland Hills at four months of age, by Ray-Mor's Adjent x Hexe of Highland Hills, owned and bred by Clare T. Matlin.

If the litter is large enough it is best to separate them into two groups, the aggressive, hearty eaters in one group, and the more timid, slower eaters in the other group. Or give extra attention to the slower ones, and see that they get enough to eat, or they will go thin and lack in substance and strength.

During hot weather, be certain that the pup has a constant supply of fresh, clean water. If water is not available at all times, provide it in quantity within an hour after feeding. There is a new lick-spout on the market, similar to the watering devices used for small laboratory animals, that will supply constant fresh water from a faucet without the necessity of pail or pan watering. The faucet to which this gadget is attached must, of necessity, be low enough so that the pup can reach it easily.

Accustom the puppies to being brushed and combed at an early age. Teach them to stand still at arms length during the procedure. An ordinary hair brush of any kind can be used for very young puppies, and a good quality wire brush and a steel comb later. For heavy shedding later on in life a hack-saw blade or a close-toothed flea comb should be employed to remove loose hair.

Don't be afraid to raise your Shepherd pup out of doors if he has a warm house to use when the weather is very cold. A dog brought up in the house living in artificial conditions of light and heat has irregular shedding periods and is much more susceptible to quick changes of temperature. The Shepherd is a strong and powerful working dog, not a lap dog, so treat him accordingly.

There are many of us who, nevertheless, want our puppy to be brought up in the house and as a house pet. This is, of course, the ideal for the one or even two dog owner. Yet, even under these circumstances, your Shepherd should have an outdoor run in which he can be put when you are absent and wish him to be outdoors. This, to your Shepherd pup, becomes his sanctuary, and it keeps him from getting into trouble. A house provided with the run will give him shelter in rain or cold.

A portable run can be used at first to give the pup or puppies exercise and sun outdoors. Such runs can be bought in all sizes and are handy to have. Or you can build your own, making it just high enough so that the pup can't get over but not too high so that it will prevent you from stepping over into the pen. Metal stakes can be used for the corner posts.

When you plan a permanent run for your Shepherd make it as large as your property will permit (within reason, that is). 20′ by 40′ is a good size for one or two dogs. It may seem awfully large for the small puppy, but he will grow into a big working dog who needs space in which to move and exercise. Provide shade in some section of the run as protection against hot summer sun. Natural shade trees are ideal and help to beautify the kennel area, but if they are not available a piece of canvas judiciously utilized can have the same effect.

A good sized house for your Shepherd puppy when he reaches full growth would be about 3 by 5 feet and about 3 feet high at the highest point. A front porch should be attached with a roof to offer shade and a dry place to lie on when the weather is bad. Insulation can be added inside and the door should be as small as possible to keep out cold air. A piece of blanket nailed over the door can keep out arctic blasts.

The best surface for an outdoor run is open to argument. Many breeders have their own pet run surface that they claim is best. The easiest to take care of is a cement surface, but it can get quite hot underfoot for a pup during the summer months. I have always recommended a cement base with building sand on top. Stools are easily removed from the sand, it packs down nicely, and periodically it can be completely removed and a new sand surface provided. It is inexpensive as a surface and the cement underneath, when the sand is removed, can be burned or the surface washed down with disinfectants to destroy worm eggs, etc.

Fencing the permanent run can be done in various ways and at different costs. Sections can be bought ready for erection, or you can use cedar posts and less expensive wire. It is up to you. Just be sure that the materials you use will not degenerate in a short time and have to be replaced. And see to it that the run wire is high enough to keep the puppy in when he's fully grown* and thick enough to hold him at maturity.

Don't bathe your pup unless it is absolutely necessary. There are many dry shampoos on the market today that, coupled with a good grooming, will generally remove any dirt and keep your puppy clean and sweet smelling. If your

*Author's note: At least six feet high and for complete safety the run should have ceiling wire.

pup gets into and is stained by paint, check the thinning agent and use it for stain removal, but remember that the agent must be removed by soap and warm water *immediately*. This is especially true of turpentine.

If you find it necessary to bathe the puppy, there are prepared, canned lathers, paste soaps that require no rinsing, and liquid detergents, all manufactured specifically for canine bathing.

Keep the puppy's toenails trimmed. This can be done with a manicure scissors while the puppy is young. Later, as the nail becomes tougher and more horny, the guillotine-type of nail clipper made especially for dogs should be used. Be careful not to cut too deeply. A flashlight held under the nail will enable you to see the dark area of the blood line so you can avoid cutting into it. If you should tap the blood supply in the nail, simply keep the pup quiet until the bleeding stops. Munsel's solution or a styptic pencil will help. A regular dog file can be used to finish the nails. If a nail has bled from trimming do not file it for at least 24 hours. File from above with a downward, rounding stroke. If you live in the city and your pup gets plenty of exercise walking on cement sidewalks, its nail growth will probably be taken care of by natural wearing off on the cement surface. If not, clipping will be in order.

Soft rib bones, dog biscuits, and some of the manufactured play-toys for puppies, will all help to prevent tartar from forming on your pup's teeth.* A puppy begins to shed his baby teeth at about 14 weeks of age. Check the mouth frequently during this period. Sometimes you will find it necessary to pull out a loose tooth, which can be done with a small pair of electrician's pliers. The gums will be swollen and painful to some extent but, unlike human babies, puppies have little trouble teething.

When you purchase a puppy and bring it home, be sure that you have everything prepared for the new addition to

---

*Author's note: Nylabone is a good and chewable product for dogs' teeth.

Arry v. Haus Schuler, C.D.X., a typey male with nine points toward his championship when this picture was taken at three years. By Ingo Wunschelrute x Irene of Cedarstone, owned by Clare T. Matlin.

your family. Have pans for food and water ready, a special place where the new arrival can sleep in peace. And let him roam throughout the house to become acquainted with it. Your Shepherd pup will not need or want a sleeping basket. A rug, away from floor drafts, will serve the purpose admirably. Until the pup is housebroken it is best to confine him to a specific area that can be easily cleaned, such as the bathroom.

Flies during the summer months can prove to be terrible pests to the Shepherd puppy (*as well as the grown Shepherd*) biting the upright or up-coming ears until they are bloody and sore. A good liquid insecticide should be rubbed or

Haidee of Ridge Hill, C.D.X. was sired by Arry, the stud at the top of the page. Out of Frieda v. Quentin, the sire's type, color and trainability was evidently transmitted to his daughter.

sprayed on the pup's ears as often as necessary for protection.

To develop the floating, easy trot that is the Shepherd dog's heritage, your pup needs lots of exercise. Puppies playing together generally get good exercise, but a pup alone depends on you for this as he must for all things. A thrown ball or stick which he is trained to chase and bring back is good exercise. Training him to jump when he gets older is also good. At about 7 months you can train him to run beside a bicycle. Make him trot and keep it up for several miles when he reaches maturity.

If you travel with the pup in hot weather, *never* leave him in a closed car in the sun alone. Death takes its grisly toll each summer of dogs so treated.

A periodic health check of your pup throughout his lifetime by your veterinarian can pay big mental and mone-

Another daughter of the sire, Arry v. Haus Schuler, C.D.X., this is Lady vom Haus Lauren, U.D., whose dam was Berna of Vanderveer, C.D.X. Intelligence and trainability are this bitch's heritage.

Above and below are puppies from the same litter, their physical relationship quite obvious. The litter was bred by Joan C. Sic, and the pups are well-grown at three months. Sired by Ilk v. Fuchteler Wald x Zsa Zsa of Twin Lance.

tary dividends. Remember to bring a sample of his stool for analysis.

We must never forget that this pup needs mental as well as physical care. Other breeds can be stuck away in a kennel and make a life for themselves, but not yours. Your pup's character and mental health needs care as much as his physical being. Give him companionship and understanding and you will be paid many times over in love and devotion.

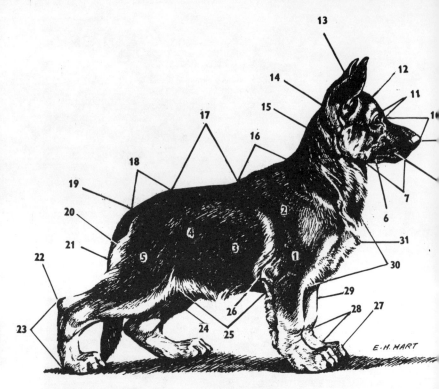

EXTERNAL ANATOMY OF THE SHEPHERD PUPPY
1. Upper arm 2. Shoulder blade 3. Ribbing 4. Loin 5. Thigh 6. Lip corner (flew) 7. Lower jaw 8. Muzzle 9. Nose 10. Foreface 11. Stop 12. Skull 13. Ears 14. Occiput 15. Crest of neck 16. Withers 17. Back 18. Croup 19. Set on of tail 20. Feathering of hindquarter 21. Tail (or stern) 22. Point of hock 23. Hock 24. Point of stifle (knee) 25. Bottom line 26. Elbow 27. Feet (paws) 28. Pastern 29. Forearm 30. Forechest 31. Prosternum (breastbone)

Chapter 6.

SELECTING THE SHEPHERD PUPPY

Time passes quickly when you watch a litter grow. If you are the breeder you have certainly not wasted that time. You have watched the puppies in the litter carefully, while they ate, while they ran around, walked and played. You have probably centered your interest on one particular puppy, or perhaps two that are difficult to choose between, for this pup or these two puppies show the greatest promise of any in the litter.

As the breeder you should know all there is to know about their genetic background, what faults and what virtues are prevalent in the strains represented by the dam and the sire you selected to produce this litter. You can look for these faults and virtues in the puppies to see if hidden recessives have linked in this breeding and become visible in the whelps.

You also have had the advantage of knowing the sire and probably have seen other of his get from different bitches so that you know what he can pass on to his puppies. Be aware also, if possible, of the *hidden* faults both of the parents can pass on to their progeny. These include obvious faults of conformation and temperament and inherited health faults that can wreak havoc later on in the form of unsuspected tendencies toward genetically linked diseases and anomalies.

The puppy you select as outstanding in the litter you will either keep, if it is of the right sex for you, or you will sell for a higher price to someone who is looking for a potential show dog.

If you are the prospective buyer of a puppy you lack the above advantages enjoyed by the breeder. But the strange

Volker v. Zollgrenzschutz-Haus, SchH. III, youth Sieger and twice mature Sieger of Germany, also World Sieger, one of the most beautiful German Shepherds ever bred and a great sire. Bred and was owned by Josef Wassermann, Germany, Volker was by Harry v. Donaukai x Perle v. Zollgrenzschutz-Haus.

part about this whole business of picking a young puppy from a litter is that the novice buyer *sometimes* stands as good a chance of getting the best pup as the experienced breeder. The reason for this seemingly incongruous statement lies in the fact that, assuming that the litter is of excellent breeding and well cared for, there may be several pups in the litter that will appear to be potential winners at eight to ten weeks of age. Also sectional growth varies in young animals, particularly in pups that will eventually attain the size of a Shepherd dog. Each pup, as an individual, will have a slightly different growth rate and exhibit change in relative sections of the body, as well as in over-all growth, from day to day.

If you are the potential purchaser of a Shepherd puppy, prepare yourself for your role by attending dog shows, visiting kennels, engaging in "Shepherd" talk with people who seem to have a solid knowledge of the subject, and reading *The German Shepherd Dog*. Observe, absorb and listen. And before you make the journey to any breeder to make your purchase, inquire into his or her background as well as into the background of their dogs. Make certain the breeders are intelligent people who had a definite purpose in making the breeding, have knowledge of the many aspects of the breed, and have a reputation for the production of excellent stock.

A very nice Reserve Winners Bitch handled by Bob Penny.

Above, Condor v. Zollgrenschutz-Haus, SchH. III, A.D. as a young dog, Junghunde Landsgruppen Sieger. Below, the same animal a year later, mature and "V-A 4", select class at the Sieger show. Note how the black coloration has receded even though the dog was almost two years old above. Condor was out of Carmen vom Sixtberg pictured on the previous page, and owned by Josef Wassermann.

Do *not* be blinded by show ring winnings. It has comparatively little to do with the knowledge and ability to breed fine animals or with the potential of the puppy you are about to purchase. If this was as important in breeding as many breeders seem to think, then the constant producing of great dogs would be merely a matter of breeding two champions together. Also don't be carried away by hysterical, adjective-happy advertisements. *Just be sure the pup comes from fine stock.*

If possible, when you go to select and buy a puppy, take along an experienced breeder, one who has been long in the "fancy" and whose knowledge you respect. This individual

A fine, young son of Condor v. Zolgrenschutz-Haus, Brix v. Afolderbach, out of Anka v. Afolderbach. Note how the strong, noble type of the line appears in the son.

cannot necessarily pick the pup that will mature into the best Shepherd in the litter, but can however, keep you from selecting an engaging youngster who exhibits obvious faults which you, as a novice, are not aware of and which quite possibly won't improve.

You will probably have decided which sex you will choose. Females will come in season twice a year and will have to be boarded or watched very carefully at these times. On the other hand they can produce puppies like themselves that can bring you gain in many ways. Females are often sweeter and more affectionate than males, and often even

Condor vom Sixtberg, SchH. II, A.D., as a young dog, before being imported by the author. Bred by Max Lipp he is by Volker v. Zollgrenzschutz-Haus x Caret v. Elfenhain, SchH. I, and represents many generations of "V" and "V-A" breeding. His photo on page 77 shows him when fully mature. Below is a fine "V" daughter in Germany, Holde vom Frickenhausl who is out of Tanka v. Zollgrenzschutz-Haus. On the facing page are two young Condor daughters in the U.S. bred by Ernest Wilck, four months old Viking Crest Stormy Sea, and three months old Viking Crest Sassi.

smarter, or perhaps I should rectify that statement in defense of my fellow males by writing instead that they are often quicker and more willing to please. Males, unlike the bitch who comes in season twice a year, are always in season and become very restless, to say the least, when females in the neighborhood are in season. Males also urinate on, and so harm, shrubbery. If you are selecting a male puppy as a potential source of income through stud fees . . . don't! He will have to develop into a superlative specimen for this purpose, and few do. Remember that there are people of means and knowledge who each year import fine, fully grown and well known stud dogs from Germany. These are the animals against which your male must compete in this area, and unless he becomes a champion who has taken his points at the biggest specialities, or becomes Grand Victor, he cannot compete as a stud dog against the top imports.

Despite all that I have just written, the author personally likes male Shepherds for their greater size and masculine nobility. The choice of sex is, of course, up to you as the potential purchaser.

Ask the breeder to separate the sexes so that you can give your full attention to the puppies that are of the sex of your choice. Normal puppies are friendly, inquisitive, lovable

creatures wanting immediate attention, so the youngster who backs away from you, who seems afraid of your outstretched hand, or who runs away and hides, should be immediately eliminated from consideration. This also applies to the pup who sulks in the corner wanting no part of the proceedings.

If it is a male puppy you are about to purchase, be sure that the testicles have descended into the scrotum, and ask the seller to guarantee this very necessary virtue. Do not handle the puppies at first. Watch them from a distance to observe their overall balance. And don't be rushed. You are about to pay cold cash for a living creature that is going to become a definite part of your family, a companion and dependant who will be with you for many years, so take your time in this all-important selection.

A good puppy will show all the structural virtues of a good adult dog, but in an exaggerated form. Watch the puppies when they trot. A good one moves with a balanced, though ungainly "bear cub" trot. Look for a long reach forward of the front legs, which indicates good front angulation. Hindquarter angulation sometimes improves with age but the bone angle of the shoulders never does. See that the prosternum (*the front point of the breast bone*) is slightly forward of the shoulders so that it projects beyond the line of the shoulder in profile.

The back should be short and straight, not roached or swayed. And, though short, the puppy must still be longer than he is high at the withers, his or her body having a stretched look as seen from the side, and this stretched appearance must come from shoulder layback, length of ribbing, profile width of thigh, and long, gentle slope of croup. It should *not* be due to the length of the back itself, or come through a long loin, for both of these faults bring another fault in their wake . . . a weakness in the back.

I should have mentioned before this that you *must* eliminate from consideration any pup that exhibits a long coat, very

pale pigmentation, large areas of white, or all-white pups. Do not be inveigled into thinking that white pups are desirable and pay a premium price for such an animal which the standard of the breed states, "A white dog or a dog with a nose that is not predominantly black, must be disqualified."

A small spot of white on the chest, a tiny touch on a toe, will usually vanish as the pup matures. Some pups are even born with a white tail tip, and this too, vanishes soon. Look for a lot of black on the puppy, for this black gradually recedes as the animal grows to maturity. The tan the pup exhibits should be of a good, rich color.

The bone exhibited by a 6 to 10 weeks old puppy is tremendous, especially in the male. This big bone is very desirable. Make sure though, that the legs are straight and end in nice, compact feet, not splayed toes.

The ribs, as mentioned before, should be well sprung and reach far back to allow a short loin. The pup should be broad across the back, loin, and croup. Croups are difficult to judge at this early age. Feel the forward edge of the pelvic bone with your fingers, then compare the length of the croup from this spot to where the tail sets on, with the overall length of the pup. This will give you some idea of the croup length.

The tail should not be set on too high for this generally indicates a future shortness of croup and is, in itself, an undesirable trait. The shoulder blades (the flat scapulas) should fit close together at the top. Place your finger between them, right at the top of the withers. The width between the blades should not be more than the width of your finger in an 8 weeks old pup.

Sometimes a puppy with extreme hindquarter angulation will appear cow-hocked, particularly when standing. This generally disappears with maturity and the strengthening of the hocks it brings. The hock itself should be short in comparison to the overall length of the hind leg, and the stifle or front part of the hind leg, when seen in profile, should show a nice curve.

Avoid the puppy that looks too finished at this early age. It will generally never gain the size and bone necessary in the adult dog. Be careful, too, of the biggest, loosest, and clumsiest pup (this is particularly seen in male puppies), for it might never attain true compactness or fluidity of movement and will probably mature into what the fancy calls a "*wet*" animal. The head should be wedge shaped and fairly broad between the ears. The eye should be dark and slightly almond shaped, never round and protruding. The eyes of young puppies are always blue, turning to their true color as they mature. Examine the teeth, mouth and jaws

Correct scissors bite, side and front views.

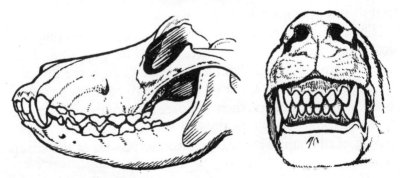

to determine the bite (articulation of the jaws and teeth), which should be a *scissors* bite. Sometimes slight anomalies in this area will right themselves with the permanent or adult teeth, but it is best not to take this chance.

Female puppies are generally smaller and daintier than male puppies, showing greater refinement in overall structure and particularly in the head. Look for rather high set ears for they generally come up without too much trouble. Ears that are heavy, thick, and hang like a hound's, are the kind that later will give you trouble.

The purpose for your selection is important. If you wish a dog to show, look for extreme angulation, high withers, rather long neck, overall balance, and style. If you wish to select a puppy that you intend to train for Schutzhund work, select a youngster of good breeding that comes from Schutzhund stock that has achieved good scores; get an eager, outgoing puppy. Character is important for both the show ring dog and the working dog. For the obedience ring, a pup of either American or German breeding will suffice so long as its temperament is sound. Conformation must, of course, *always* be good. Do not buy a puppy as a pet and then later decide to show it. That just doesn't work. German dogs have been bred for nearly a century for utilitarian purpose, to do a job of work. American-bred dogs have been genetically fashioned for the show ring or to produce pets.

With your purchased puppy you will receive, indeed you must *insist* upon receiving, certain documents, these include; a bill of sale that guarantees that the puppy is free from disease and in the best of health, a guarantee that the puppy's ears will stand erect in time, and that it is free from hip dysplasia* (sometimes also called subluxation, a disease of the hips prevalent in German Shepherds as well as many other breeds), that, if a male, it is sexually whole (meaning that both testicles have descended) and not a crypt or

---

*Author's note: This guarantee is optional and is entirely up to the seller and buyer.

monorchid, a three generation pedigree, and the puppy's A.K.C. registration slip.

For your part you will have to keep the puppy isolated from contact with other puppies or dogs for a week to ten days so that it will not be exposed to any disease carried by another animal. The reason for this time limit is because most canine illnesses have an incubation period of from 5 to 10 days. It is a wise precaution, though, directly after purchase, to bring the pup to the veterinarian for a complete examination and to arrange to protect the puppy and give him immunity from certain very lethal diseases through vaccination. The breeder should have supplied you with a health certificate designating what worming, vaccinations, etc., the puppy has been given. Do not forget to bring with you to the veterinarian's a sample of the pup's stool.

Remember this when you purchase a puppy: the initial cost is little in comparison to what it will cost you to feed the animal all its life and keep it healthy and happy. So don't be afraid to spend that extra $25 for a better puppy.

Incidentally, teething will often cause the puppy's ears to droop down after they have been standing erect. If this happens, you can safely assume that once he has finished teething the ears will again erect themselves.

The trouble with all the guarantees that I have advised you to get with your Shepherd pup is that if they are not fulfilled as the pup develops, and even if the integrity of the seller is such that he firmly stands behind his guarantees, it will probably still be too late for you, the purchaser. The reason for this lies in your emotional humanness. The puppy has wound himself around your heart and you, after having it with you and loving and caring for it, can not give it up, no matter what faults it develops.

Remember *always* to give your pup the opportunity to develop the character and intelligence for which the German Shepherd is justly famed, and that has made him such a fine helpmate to mankind in so many utilitarian categories.

Chapter 7.

TRAINING THE SHEPHERD PUPPY

All puppies must be trained so that they will conduct themselves in the manner expected of such well-born individuals. We are indeed lucky in that our pupil is of a breed of acknowledged superior intelligence. During this early training period when you are shaping the character and intelligence of your puppy into specific patterns of behavior, you will also be fashioning a relationship between you and your dog that will endure throughout his lifetime. You give the commands, and your puppy *must* obey. This is the simple formula for training.

The author does *not* believe in punishment as a means of training. I do believe in the reward system, but the reward I advocate does not necessarily need to be a tidbit or any such bribe to the primary senses. A pat, a smile, a *"well done"*, by his master is quite often all the reward that the puppy needs. With some pups, or under some circumstances, the tidbit reward may be necessary or desirable, and should then be used. But physical punishment, beating, whipping, or hurting the pup, is the act of a sadist and such a person should not train a dog, rather should they train themselves.

Actually, using your hand, the leash, a broom, rolled up newspaper, or any other vehicle of punishment to show your displeasure to the puppy for any act he has committed, results in his fear of the object and of the act of training itself. If you slap and hurt him with your hand he will very likely become hand-shy. He can become leash-shy, broom-shy, etc., with the use of such objects by you, to hurt him while conveying your displeasure. Rolled up newspaper as a vehicle of punishment can make it impossible to housebreak him to paper, or can result in his attacking the paperboy at some later date.

The only reason for striking a dog is if he, with malice aforethought, bites. The only other reason to mete out physical pain is when, after all other methods fail, you must break your dog of car chasing. Then the water pistol with a weak solution of ammonia and water can be employed with the knowledge that it will certainly discomfort the dog but, with possible death as an alternative, is definitely the better of two evils.

Except for the above reasons, there is no excuse for using physical violence during the act of training a dog unless it is

Amer. Ch. Amigo v. Land der Berge SchH. III. Imported by Heidi and David Landau of Von Furstenberg Shepherds. The author gave this handsome male Best of Breed to finish his Championship in Miami. Handled by Jimmy Moses.

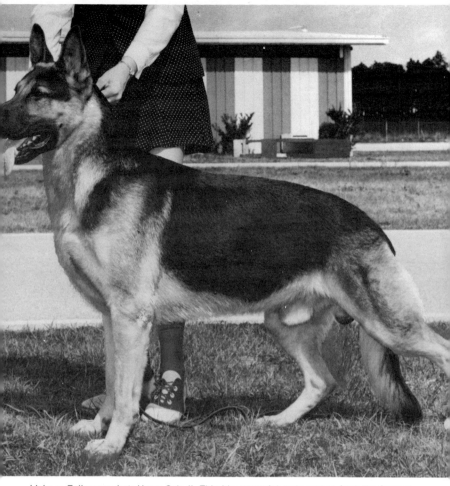

Lieko v. Zollgrenzschutz-Haus, Sch. II. This big, powerful male comes from the famous kennel of Josef Wassermann in Germany. He was owned by Jim and Carol Sheridan.

your last recourse and, if this is so, then you must face the fact that you, not your dog, have failed, and that you are not able or fit to train a dog.

When you train a dog you do two things; you exert your will over the puppy and his actions and, in so doing, you *control* his conduct (*the word "control" is the important element here*). Secondly you *condition* the puppy to react to specific external stimuli.

The author working his schutzhund import on the sleeve. The dog is Etzel v. Burgrain, SchH. III, A.D.

The secret of complete control is *firmness*. Always be firm and insist that the puppy obey once he understands what it is you want him to do. The basis upon which the conditioning of the puppy to perform certain acts is founded is through exact and constant repetition of the stimulating factor. In other words, when you condition a puppy to perform a certain action through a command you have given him, you are causing him to form a *habit pattern* to which he will react automatically whenever he hears that specific command. But, to achieve exact results, the conditioning factor, the command, must always be the same, never varying in structure or tone. Therefore, if the command is, *"Come, Duke!"* never vary it to *"Here, Duke!"*, *"Come on!"* or any other grouping of words or sounds that mean the same thing to you . . . they won't to the pup. The command must always be, *"Come, Duke!"*, delivered in the same way with the *identical* tonal quality each time issued.

Other important elements of training are; keep training periods short, lengthen the time as the puppy grows older and has absorbed other commands. Use sharp, short, easily understood words of command. Approach the training period seriously. Have a definite time for it when there will be no interruptions. Select a training place where there is no outside activity that can steal the pup's attention from his training. Censure the pup in a rebuking tone when he doesn't obey, and praise him, or reward him with a tidbit, when he obeys promptly.

With quiet patience and authority, take your novice through a specific training maneuver repeatedly until he performs it correctly, then praise him. Every movement you make in training must be smooth and exact, and the pupil must eventually obey promptly. You can, during these early training sessions, lay the foundation for later obedience or Schutzhund work.

The equipment necessary to train your pup is simple, unless you become enamored of obedience work and go on to advanced training. You will need a light chain choke collar and a long leash.

But, before you begin any formal training you can lay the basis for the pup's later deportment through the very important and initial job of puppy training, *housebreaking*. For this chore you need no collar or leash, merely knowledge and patience.

You will need to know that puppies urinate very soon after drinking milk or water, and when they are brought into a warm room, particularly if brought from an area where it is colder. They will also wet directly after they have been awakened. Puppies defecate generally within a half hour after eating.

You will have to patiently watch the puppy until you become aware of the warning signs and movements that precede evacuation. When you see these signs pick the pup up *immediately* and rush him to the place you have assigned for these duties, indoors or out.

When the pup, by accident or design, goes where you want him to, praise him extravagantly. Should he make one of his frequent mistakes, scold him, using both your voice and its tone to impart your displeasure. The simple word "*No!*" is adequate and a word he should learn and obey in diverse other circumstances during training. "*Good boy*", or "*Good girl*", as the case may be, delivered in an excruciatingly pleased voice, conveys your praise.

Whatever the material used underfoot in the whelping box or nest will be the substance upon which the puppy has learned to go and will seek afterward for this same purpose. Thus a puppy conditioned to go on paper in the nest will seek paper when out of the nest on which to do his duty, and will be readily paper-broken. If hay or straw was used in the whelping box it will be much easier to teach the puppy to go outdoors on grass. Usually Shepherd puppies spend the first early weeks of their lives on hay, straw or a similar material, and usually, in fact when one considers the eventual size of the breed, necessarily, the puppy is housebroken to use the great outdoors. Shepherd owners are fortunate in the fact that, as a breed, a Shepherd is naturally clean in its habits and easily housebroken. As a matter of fact many Shepherds raised in an outside run never have to be deliberately housebroken, preferring to use the ground for their act and sensing the fact that the house is not to be soiled.

Take the puppy outside after eating, waking, drinking, etc., and stay with him until he relieves himself, then praise him. Puppies, and grown dogs, too, prefer to defecate in places other dogs have used, or where they have relieved themselves before. So if you take him to the same place every time, he will relieve himself readily.

Assuming that he makes a mistake in the house, admonish him with a sharp vehement, and agonizing, "*No!*" or a grief stricken, "*Shame!*" and immediately remove him to the area you wish him to use. *Never* push his nose in his excreta as a form of punishment or training, and *never* scold him unless you catch him in the act. A few seconds after he has performed any act for which he should be

Zando of Twin Lance at ten weeks, by Aro Zur Geigerklause x Sarego's Quality, owned and bred by Charles Griffin.

The same pup, Zando, at three and a half months of age. Note how the black pigmentation is receding.

Zando at eighteen months, fully grown and handsome but not yet completely mature. The gold coloration has spread, leaving only the saddle and muzzle black, plus head and shoulder bands.

chastised he will have forgotten all about it and punishment will only bewilder him, because he will not have the slightest idea why he is being chastised.

If a paper-broken puppy is to be trained to go outdoors, simply remove the *soiled* paper from the house, anchor it outdoors with stones so that it will not blow away, and bring your puppy to it. Once he begins to use it outside, you must commence cutting down on its size until nothing of it is left after a period of 8 to 10 days, and the pup is using the bare ground.

A lot of grief can be avoided by confining the pup to one room until he is thoroughly housebroken, particularly at

Hammer v. Zollgrenzschutz-Haus, SchH. II; sire: Int. Eur. Ch. Held v. Flosser-haus ScH. III; dam: Chuna v. Zollgrenzschutz-Haus. This big stud was linebred on World Sieger Volker v. Zollgrenzschutz-Haus and was owned by the author.

night. This should be a room with a linoleum or tile floor for easy cleaning, probably the bathroom. If he is house-broken during the day but makes mistakes at night, tie him close to his bed, or confine him to a dog house within the room; few dogs will soil their beds or sleeping quarters. If you must leave the pup alone for any length of time, con-fine him to a limited area which includes his bed and the paper or box.

The use of human baby suppositories can aid you in timing the evacuation process and controlling that time. Injection of the suppository generally brings quick results.

Another trick used in paper breaking is to confine the pup to a small room and cover the floor with paper. After he has formed the habit of going on the paper begin to remove a piece day by day until only one piece remains. This can then be taken beyond the room with a closed door in between and only a small edge of the paper projecting into the pup's room. The pup wanting to go, will see the edge of paper and begin to whine and he will be, as of that moment, housebroken to paper wherever you wish to place it.

Assuming that the puppy is housebroken let us now return to the area of training deportment. Our first task will be to collar and leash train the puppy. To this end you

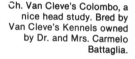

Ch. Van Cleve's Colombo, a nice head study. Bred by Van Cleve's Kennels owned by Dr. and Mrs. Carmelo Battaglia.

must purchase a narrow, cheap, flat leather collar and allow him to wear it constantly and become used to it. After a day or two attach a piece of cord to the collar long enough to reach the ground. Don't let him play with the cord, just let him drag it around and become accustomed to it so that he will be partially leash-broken by the time you attach the leash and gently lead him about.

Once he accepts collar and leash, replace the leather collar with the chain choke collar and make him follow you when on leash, using short, gentle jerks to make him follow and move with you. Call his name to get his attention, then

The author using the "whirling leash" technique to teach the pupil to "Heel" properly. If the dog forges out ahead the whirling leash taps its nose causing it to return to the "Heel" position.

add the word, "*Heel!*" Soon he will trot along freely at your left side (*always on your left side*) on a loose leash, and you will be praising him with the inevitable, "*Good boy!*"

Every time you feed your pup, call him with a "*Come!*". Eating is a pleasurable experience and you are conditioning him to come to you freely. When you urge your puppy to "come" to his pan for feeding (a pleasurable experience) and have prefixed the call with his name, you are conditioning him to come immediately when called, you have therefore begun an important part of his basic training. Later, with a long leash attached to his collar, get as far away from him as the length of the leash and call, "*Come!*" and in no time he will respond. It is generally best to preface every command with the use of the pup's name. He learns his name early and by using it in this manner you immediately catch his attention. Always use short jerks on the leash, never a long pull.

To make the puppy sit, hold your hand under his chin to prop up his foreparts and with your other hand press down on his rump forcing his hindquarters to go down, at the

The correct positions of hands and leash in teaching the dog to "Sit"; hold the front end up and push the rear end down.

The pupil in the "Sit" position at the instructor's side, being given the hand signal to "Stay".

Clare Matlin's, Val, at eighteen months of age in a perfect "Sit" position awaiting a new command.

Working free of the leash, the dog has been recalled by the author and has assumed the front "Sit" position before being given the "heel" command for the finish. Below, the "Down" signal accompanying the oral command, with the pupil on leash.

At left, working free and from a distance, the "Sit" signal. Below, the "Down" signal drops the dog in his tracks while he is obeying the oral recall to "Come".

same time, using the vocal command "*Peter, sit!*" Augment this positive training by using the same command quietly whenever you see the pup about to sit of its own accord.

Once trained to "*sit*" upon command, both positive and negative approaches can be utilized to teach him to lie down. Here the command is "*Down!*" and the puppy, already in the "*Sit*" position is either pushed down in front or the front legs pulled forward so that the forepart lowers to the ground or floor. Again the negative approach can be utilized through observation and taking advantage of the pup's natural inclination to lie down and giving him the command when he does.

When you have housebroken your puppy, trained him to "*come*", "*heel*", "*sit*", and "*down*" upon command, you have accomplished all you can until you begin serious training when he is about 6 months of age. For this advanced training the author recommends that a book on training be purchased that is devoted wholly, not in part as is this book, to that important subject.*

All that you have read in this chapter in reference to training is basic, specifically aimed at training the young puppy; a sort of kindergarten course. That is why the "*sit*" and "*down*" commands can be taught off leash. When serious training begins with the older puppy, the leash is always used until advancement has been such that the dog will work accurately and with verve and dependability off leash. Teaching the very young puppy the necessary few basic commands should not be done with the grim, rigid, business-like air employed later in serious training. The puppy should nevertheless obey the simple commands with alacrity once they are learned, for you are establishing, in these tender weeks, the control necessary for earnest training to come.

*DOG TRAINING, by Lew Burke, published by T.F.H. Publications, is recommended.

Later, with the puppy leashed and at your left side, the act of training him to "*sit*", "*heel*", "*down*", etc., will be an accomplished fact and only promptness and precision must be learned. This also helps the pupil to move with ease into the much more rigid regime of real training for he already knows how to perform some of the acts and he has been conditioned to obey, and to be controlled by your voice and will, to perform certain exercises.

Remember that your shepherd puppy will mature into a large sized working dog and he must be trained to be under

Ch. Britmere's Timothy of Lahngold, by Treu v. Wolfs-stock (imported) x Lahngold's Vodka, photo taken at sixteen months. This beautifully balanced, richly pigmented young male was a fine sire and show dog. Timothy was bred by Ernest Loeb and was owned by Bob Andrews.

Ch. Covy's Felita of Tucker Hill ROM. Another one of the grand animals bred by Gloria Birch and Cappy Pottle at Covy-Tucker Hill Kennels.

control at all times. Shepherds are born and bred to work and love it. So train your dog and give him the opportunity to work for you.

If you are interested in more advanced training, I recommend that you join training classes for obedience or Schutzhund work, whichever you desire. Obedience training will fashion your dog into a well trained and obedient solid citizen that you can take anywhere. Schutzhund training will produce an animal highly trained in tracking, obedience, and protection. Both forms of training will bring a rapport and closeness between you and your dog that is beyond price. And Schutzhund training will make him a well controlled protector, a designation very much desired in this era of rampant crime.

A very handsome head study of a very handsome male, Ch. Britmere's Timothy of Lahngold.

Chapter 8.

THE SHEPHERD PUPPY'S HEALTH

Let me make something clear at the beginning of this chapter; you are not a veterinarian and therefore you are not really capable of treating your puppy for illness any more than you, a layman, are capable of treating your child when it is sick. But, there are many ways in which you can help your pup retain its health, and it is important that you are cognizant of the symptoms of disease and ill-health so that treatment can begin in time.

IMMUNITY AND VACCINATIONS

Your puppy's skin is the initial barrier against disease. Antibodies protect him from antigens, foreign proteins causing a

A six weeks old daughter of Timothy's, Bee Jay's Touche, owned and bred by Betty J. Irwin.

variety of physical ailments. The immunity your puppy develops depends upon its inherited ability to protect its body from the invasion of antigens, and quite frequently that ability breaks down. One thing you must remember. . .*immunity against any disease does not last a lifetime.*

Your Shepherd is born with some immunities, but he must be protected from disease before these immunities disappear. This is the time when your veterinarian must vaccinate him against the most destructive of canine diseases: Distemper, Hepatitis, Leptospirosis, Rabies, and Parvovirus.

Infectious hepatitis, primary encephalitis, and a great many other diseases formerly had been diagnosed as distemper. With more accurate diagnosis, great strides have been made in conquering not only distemper, but these other, allied diseases. Distemper (Carre) is still prevalent in spite of successful methods of immunization. In many instances, even if the dog gets well, he will be left with some dreadful souvenir of the disease which will mar him for life. After-effects are common in most of the diseases of the distemper complex.

Distemper (Carre's Disease) is exceedingly deadly, and the virus is spread by a dozen different means. Diarrhea, mucous discharge from eyes and nose, vomiting, convulsions, hind-quarter collapse and tremors are symptoms that lead to death.

Hepatitis (Rubarth's Disease) resembles distemper in its effects. It attacks the liver and causes jaundice, congestion, and swelling around the head. Live vaccines are used for both Distemper and Hepatitis. The newest vaccine, Adenovirus type 2, produces less reaction and also protects against other respiratory viruses.

Leptospirosis (Weill's or Stuttgart's Disease) is transferred to the dog through urine. There are two kinds that affect dogs, and the initial carriers of this bacterial disease are rats. The spirochete assaults the liver, kidneys, intestinal tract, peri-

A fine male puppy being awarded best puppy by the author in a California Specialty. Jack LaRue handling.

98

toneum and pleura. The coat is dry, the temperature high, there is vomiting, evidence of kidney damage, and the mucous membranes become jaundiced. Both types of leptospirosis are controlled by the vaccine, but protection is often limited.

Specific vaccines may be employed by your veterinarian as a preventive measure. Initial diagnosis is difficult, and the disease has generally made drastic inroads before a cure is effected. It has been estimated that fully 50 percent of all dogs throughout the world have been stricken with leptospirosis at one time or another and that in many instances the disease was not recognized for what it was. The disease produced by Leptospira in the blood of humans is known as Weil's disease.

Rabies can affect all mammals, including man. It is a particularly dreadful disease, culminating in death. It is a viral disease, and control through the medium of vaccination is imperative. The diseased animal can transfer the virus through its saliva into any open wound, where it enters the body of the victim and travels to the brain through the nervous system.

The rabid animal shows a definite change in behavior; it exhibits excess saliva, quits eating and drinking, and crawls into dark, quiet places. After a few days it enters either a paralytic form that leads to its demise or a "furious" form that causes it to become a "mad dog," attacking everything and fearing nothing. Finally there are convulsions and death.

Inoculation is generally given after your Shepherd is six months old.

Parvovirus is an extremely deadly and contagious disease in dogs. Modified live parvo vaccine is the most effective. This malady attacks the intestinal tract and causes high fever, lethargy, appetite loss, bloody diarrhea and vomiting. Small puppies stricken with this disease become dead victims within two hours.

Parainfluenza. Vaccination for this disease negates the effect of "kennel cough," a virulent illness in the disease complex. Puppies that are vaccinated are more responsive to treatment and more easily treated for the ailment.

Above: The author judging in the Dominican Republic Shepherd Specialty Show. This is the Winners Male. **Below:** Ch. Steinhugel's Siggo being awarded Best of Breed by the author. Owned by Anne Given and handled here by Jack LaRue. A Major win at a large specialty.

Measles Vaccine is derived from human measles virus. Distemper virus and measles virus are "look-alikes," and the antibodies give cross-protection. The vaccine is used to combat distemper in young puppies whose natural antibodies (derived from the dam's milk) might block the effectiveness of distemper vaccine. It should only be used on puppies in the five- to seven-week-old span.

Injections for distemper, etc. should be started at about 9 weeks. Vaccines do not affect the tissues, nor do they cause any ill effects to other dogs who come in contact with the vaccinated animal.

Two puppies out of the same dam, the sable Panthre's Delight of Delilah. The three weeks old Mindy of Fran-Jo on the left is sired by Ch. Field Marshal of Arbywood. Donna of Fran-Jo, shown at two and a half months, is by Ch. Lance of Fran-Jo.

External Parasites

Fleas can act as an intermediate host for heartworm; they also can carry tapeworm to your puppy. Allergy to flea saliva can cause canine skin diseases. Lice and ticks can also inhabit your pet and make him ill as well as irritated; external parasites must be decimated.

There are powders, sprays, dips and flea collars to protect your pup. Use several kinds in your battle against these pernicious pests, for they seem to eventually become immune to any one particular eradicator. Your veterinarian and pet dealer can advise you about the best products to use.

Internal Parasites

Worms or their eggs can be ingested by your pup, or they can penetrate his skin. Your dog can become infested through an insect bite or from prenatal infection. From a stool examination your veterinarian will be able to pinpoint the species of worm infesting your puppy.

Roundworms. There are two species of roundworms that can infest the small intestines of your Shepherd puppy, and they are much more dangerous to puppies than to grown dogs. They can both be eliminated with piperazine compounds, which are mild, require no period of starvation.

Hookworms are hair-thin and also infest the intestines, but they are generally much more dangerous to your pup's health than roundworms. Hookworms are tiny vampires that suck the dog's blood; they cause diarrhea and anemia and, if not eliminated, can cause puppy deaths.

Whipworms are found in the caecum and the large intestine. If not eliminated, they can lead to death.

Tapeworm. There are a great variety of tapeworms that can affect your puppy; they range from one inch long to 16 feet in length. They require several intermediate hosts to complete their life cycle.

Yomesan and Dicarbil are the drugs commonly used to eradicate tapeworms. Roundworms, hookworms, and whipworms can also be treated with Panacur. Remember your pup must be wormed more than once, the timing reflecting the life cycle of the specific helminth.

Heartworms can reach a foot in length and cram the heart, lungs, pulmonary arteries and the large veins. Mosquitoes are the carrying hosts. Treatment is through either surgery or the use of arsenical drugs and antimony.

Prevention is much more important and is accomplished through the use of Decacide tablets (Diethylcarbamazine citrate), one 400 mg. tablet a day for an adult German Shepherd. Preventive treatment must *not* be given to dogs that harbor adult heartworms.

Another disease, *coccidiosis*, caused by a tiny protozoan, is also very dangerous to puppies. A severe case often proves fatal. Loose and bloody stools as well as general unthriftiness is indicative of the presence of this disease. The reason coccidiosis is so dangerous is because the puppy is infected over and over again. Strict sanitation and supportive treatment of good nutrition, utilizing fat, milk, bone ash and kaopectate, with added dextrose and calcium is important and necessary as supportive treatment. Nitroforazone administered every 8 hours for 10 days or more is excellent, and fragmentary clinical evidence seems to indicate that sulfamethazine may give some control over canine coccidiosis.

Skin Diseases

Often difficult to diagnose, skin diseases can take months to cure. There are frequently contributing factors such as a reaction to flea saliva and other allergenic materials, thyroid imbalance, and irritation of the sites by scratching and biting. The skin of the dog borders on the alkaline, not acid, as is the skin of humans. Therefore special soaps manufactured specifically for dogs must be used for cleansing and treating skin diseases.

Mange is a skin disease that is characterized by constant scratching; because of infection and lesions, identification is not always absolute. There are two forms of mange affecting dogs, sarcoptic and demodectic. Medicated baths, insecticides in a soothing base and adjunctive therapy are essential to a cure. Follow your veterinarian's advice.

Skin diseases, other than those caused by mange mites, are the eczemas and ringworm. Ringworm is a fungus infection and is contagious to humans (athletes foot is ringworm infection). In puppies ringworm generally appears as a round or oval spot from which the hair has fallen. Iodine glycerine or an internal fungicide such as girseofulvin are definite cures for this condition. Of recent origin is a new drug to retard the spread of, and to cure, fungus. It is a

Nixe a.d. Eremitenklause, SchH. I, a top German show bitch and producer, she had the same breeding as Klodo a.d. Eremitenklause, a breeding repeated many times in Germany.

locally applied fungicide named Tinactin, is colorless, odorless, stainless and liquid and seems to be equally effective against almost every form of fungus infection.

Eczema is probably a syndrome rather than a disease. It spreads rapidly from raw, wet spots that the dog licks and inflames by scratching. Bacterial infection follows, and you soon have a mixed bag of skin diseases.

You must first find and treat the underlying cause. You must then treat the affected areas and stop the itching.

A fine, big boned, five months old male puppy in Germany, Xello a.d. Eremitenklause, out of the bitch Nixe, above and sired by Jacko v. Bimohlen.

105

Specific medication must be applied to the basic cause once it has been identified, then corticosteroids will reduce the itch and topical ointments aid in healing. Lotions, ointments, and medicated baths will all help, and total flea control is essential.

General Skin Diseases

Actually skin diseases are usually specific and not general, but if your dog exhibits a skin condition, try bathing him with Thiomar, a deodorant, healing and cleansing tar shampoo. For dry, scaly skin use Derma-Oil Shampoo, Humilac, or Allergroom. Betespan Aqueous Solution (by injection) can help to alleviate constant scratching, and a Hydrocortisone liquid, H/B 101, applied to the sores can speed healing. Oxacillin, a broad-spectrum antibiotic given orally, two capsules three times a day for a grown Shepherd, can aid in recovery.

Ask your veterinarian to do a skin scrape and a blood profile, as the skin scrape can pinpoint the skin diseases.

Other Ailments

Hip Dysplasia and the extent of the joint damage and arthritic involvement can only be ascertained by X-ray. Aspirin and steroids can help to control the arthritic pain in mild cases, and surgical cutting of the pectineus muscle will relieve pressure on the joint. Removal of the femoral head and the formation of a new muscle joint returns from 80 to 90 percent normal function to the animal. Hip dysplasia is an inherited condition.

Spondylitis (spinal cord degeneration) is a paralyzing disease identified with German Shepherds. After the dog is five or six years old an unsteady gait indicates spinal cord degeneration. Incessant stretching of the hindquarters is another sign of the disease. Generally the condition stabilizes and mobility returns within reason. There is no known cure at this time.

Ear Infections. Severe head-shaking and holding the head at an odd angle are signs of ear infection. Keep the ears clean. If the infection becomes really bad, pour a capful of hydrogen

Rickets in a Shepherd puppy the result of a dietary deficiency.

peroxide into the ear and follow with Panolog Ointment, squirted deep into the ear canal.

Bloat (acute gastric dilation) is not as prevalent in Shepherds as in some other breeds. There are two kinds, Simple Bloat (dilation) and Gastric Torsion.

The first named type can be treated as outlined briefly in the first-aid treatment chart. The second, Gastric Torsion, is also called "Twisted stomach" because the stomach can turn 180 degrees, closing itself off. Only surgical intervention can save the animal, and even then the prognosis is grave. The Parasympathomimetic drugs and stomach tubing are particularly successful for simple bloat. At the moment the best drug seems to be Coecolysin, imported from West Germany.

Fits in pups are symptoms of disease rather than illness itself. Your veterinarian should be consulted. *Diarrhea* can also be included in this category as a symptom rather than a disease. If only a simple intestinal disturbance a tightening agent such as Kaopectate should be given along with boiled rice, hard boiled eggs, bone ash, kibbles, crackers or dog biscuits. Withhold water and substitute corn syrup dissolved in boiled milk to prevent dehydration.

Constipation is generally caused by diet. Introduce laxative elements into the diet such as, stewed tomatoes, buttermilk, whey, bran, etc., and a bland physic such as milk of magnesia should be given.

If your puppy is stung by wasps, you can afford the poor animal fairly quick relief and a reduction of the accompanying swelling by immediately applying vinegar to the area and cold compresses. The acid in the wasp's sting is neutralized by the acetic acid in the vinegar. Baking soda can be applied later for more complete recovery. If swelling persists and the dog is uncomfortable or in pain, take it to your veterinarian immediately.

Administering Medicine

To adminster liquid medicine make the puppy sit, raise his head and you will find a pocket at the corner of his mouth. Hold the pocket open and pour the medication in. A small bottle used as a vehicle for the dosage makes accomplishment easier.

To administer pills again raise the head of the patient and, by putting pressure on the cheeks of the pup just behind the lip edges where the teeth come together inside the mouth, force the mouth to open. Push the pills down the throat as far as possible, using the eraser end of a pencil if necessary, then quickly shut the mouth and hold it shut firmly but not too tightly. When the tip of the tongue emerges from the front of the pup's mouth you will know that the pills have been swallowed.

An ordinary rectal thermometer can be used to take your dog's temperature. The arrow that points to normal human temperature, 98.6 degrees, should be disregarded. Normal puppy temperature varies between $101\frac{1}{2}$ to 102 degrees, and sometimes higher if the pup is excited. Normal temperature for a grown dog is 101 degrees.

In applying ointment to the eye, simply pull the lower lid out and squeeze a small amount of ointment into the pocket thus produced.

If your pup becomes badly injured, quickly snap a leash on his collar and get him to your veterinarian as fast as you can. Prompt action by you and your veterinarian can save the life of the puppy that has become so much a part of your life.

There are many other diseases that your pup is heir to, but it would take another large book to discuss them. Those that I have written of are the most common ailments suffered by German Shepherds.

Before ending this chapter I must, if I am to retain your confidence, mention the hereditary and congenital diseases that can specifically affect your German Shepherd. Because of close inbreeding and linebreeding, these troublesome, genetically linked illnesses and anomalies have become more prevalent.

Hip dysplasia, already discussed, has polygenic inheritance; persistent right aortal arch in German Shepherds is congenital. Hemophilia A, factor VIII deficiency is inherited as an autosomal recessive trait, and cleft lip and cleft palate involve genetic factors. Thyroid imbalance is inherited, cryptorchidism (and monorchidism) is a sex-linked recessive, and Von Willebrand's disease (pseudo-hemophilia) is a hereditary illness. Bilateral cataracts are genetically dominant, Pannus has a genetic base, enostenosis (pain and intermittent lameness between the ages of 6 to 12 months in Shepherds, with subsequent recovery) has genetic overtones, and behavioral abnormalities are polygenic in origin. The tendency in Shepherds to bloat, early senility, and a shortened life are all also inherited characteristics, and there are many more that have not yet been catalogued.

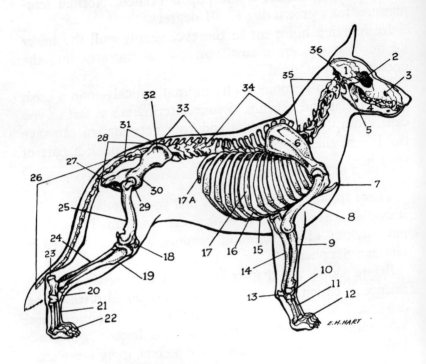

SKELETON OF A GERMAN SHEPHERD

1. Cranium (skull) 2. Orbital cavity 3. Nasal bone 4. Mandible (jaw bone) 5. Condyle 6. Scapula (shoulder blade, including spine and acromion process of scapula) 7. Prosternum 8. Humerus (upper arm) 9. Radius (front forearm bone—see Ulna) 10. Carpus (pastern joint. Comprising seven bones) 11. Metacarpus (pastern. Comprising five bones) 12. Phalanges (digits or toes) 13. Pisiform (accessory carpal bone) 14. Ulna 15. Sternum 16. Costal cartilage (lower, cartilaginous section of ribs) 17. Rib bones 17a. Floating rib (not connected by costal cartilage to sternum) 18. Patella (knee joint) 19. Tibia (with fibula comprises shank bone) 20. Tarsus (comprising seven bones 21. Metatarsus (comprising five bones) 22. Phalanges (toes or digits of hind foot) 23. Oscalcis (point of hock) 24. Fibula 25. Femur (thigh bone) 26. Coccygeal vertebra (bones of tail. Number varies—18 to 23 normal) 27. Pubis 28. Pelvic bone entire (pubis, ilium, ischium) 29. Head of femur 30. Ischium 31. Sacral vertebra (comprising five fused vertebra) 32. Ilium 33. Lumber vertebra 34. Thoracic vertebra (dorsal, with spinal process or withers) 35. Cervical vertebra (bones of the neck) 36. Occiput.

Chapter 9.

THE A.K.C. STANDARD OF THE GERMAN SHEPHERD DOG

(The standard was approved February 11, 1978.)

GENERAL APPEARANCE

The first impression of a good German Shepherd dog is that of a strong, agile, well-muscled animal, alert and full of life. It is well balanced, with harmonious development of the forequarter and hindquarter. The dog is longer than tall, deep bodied, and presents an outline of smooth curves rather than angles. It looks substantial and not spindly, giving the impression, both at rest and in motion, of muscular fitness and nimbleness without any look of clumsiness or soft living. The ideal dog is stamped with a look of quality and nobility—difficult to define, but unmistakable when present. Secondary sex characteristics are strongly marked, and every animal gives a definite impression of masculinity or femininity, according to its sex.

CHARACTER

The breed has a distinct personality marked by direct and fearless, but not hostile, expression, self-confidence and a certain aloofness that does not lend itself to immediate and indiscriminate friendships. The dog must be approachable, quietly standing its ground and showing confidence and willingness to meet overtures without itself making them. It is poised, but when the occasion demands, eager and alert; both fit and willing to serve in its capacity as companion, watchdog, blind leader, herding dog, or guardian, whichever the circum-

Owned by James Vogel, these healthy, happy puppies may some day become stars of the show ring, or perhaps fulfill their destinies as companions or guards of their master's household.

stances may demand. The dog must not be timid, shrinking behind its master or handler; it should not be nervous, looking about or upward with anxious expression or showing nervous reaction, such as tucking of tail, to strange sounds or sights. Lack of confidence under any surroundings is not typical of good character.

Any of the above deficiencies in character which indicate shyness must be penalized as very serious faults and any dog exhibiting pronounced indications of these must be excused from the ring. It must be possible for the judge to observe the teeth and to determine that both testicles are descended. Any dog that attempts to bite the judge must be disqualified. The ideal dog is a working animal with an incorruptible character combined with body and gait suitable for the arduous work that constitutes its primary purpose.

HEAD

The head is noble, cleanly chiseled, strong without coarseness, but above all not fine, and in proportion to the body. The head of the male is distinctly masculine, and that of the bitch distinctly feminine. The muzzle is long and strong with the lips firmly fitted, and its topline is parallel to the topline of the skull. Seen from the front, the forehead is only moderately arched, and the skull slopes into the long, wedge-shaped muzzle without abrupt stop. Jaws are strongly developed. *Ears:* Ears are moderately pointed, in proportion to the skull, open toward the front, and carried erect when at attention, the ideal carriage being one in which the center lines of the ears, viewed from the front, are parallel to each other and perpendicular to the ground. A dog with cropped or hanging ears must be disqualified. *Eyes:* Of medium size, almond shaped, set a little obliquely and not protruding. The color is as dark as possible. The expression keen, intelligent and composed. *Teeth:* 42 in number—20 upper and 22 lower—are strongly developed and meet in a scissors bite in which part of the inner surface of the upper incisors meet and engage part of the

The ideal German Shepherd male.

outer surface of the lower incisors. An overshot jaw or a level bite is undesirable. An undershot jaw is a disqualifying fault. Complete dentition is to be preferred. Any missing teeth other than first premolars is a serious fault.

NECK

The neck is strong and muscular, clean-cut and relatively long, proportionate in size to the head and without loose folds of skin. When the dog is at attention or excited, the head is raised and the neck carried high; otherwise typical carriage of the head is forward rather than up and but little higher than the top of the shoulders, particularly in motion.

FOREQUARTERS

The shoulder blades are long and obliquely angled, laid on flat and not placed forward. The upper arm joins the shoulder

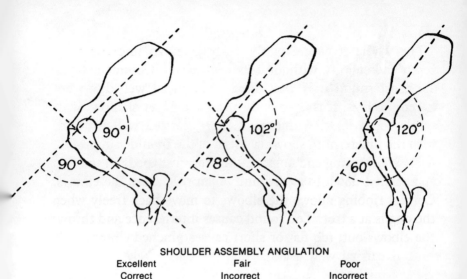

SHOULDER ASSEMBLY ANGULATION

Excellent	Fair	Poor
Correct	Incorrect	Incorrect

(extension of reach is indicated by broken lines)

blade at about a right angle. Both the upper arm and the shoulder blade are well muscled. The forelegs, viewed from all sides, are straight and the bone oval rather than round. The pasterns are strong and springy and angulated at approximately a 25-degree angle from the vertical.

FEET

The feet are short, compact, with toes well arched, pads thick and firm, nails short and dark. The dewclaws, if any, should be removed from the hind legs. Dewclaws on the front legs may be removed, but are normally left on.

PROPORTION

The German Shepherd is longer than tall, with the most desirable proportion as 10 is to 8½. The desired height for males at the highest point of the shoulder blade is 24 to 26 inches; and for bitches, 22 to 24 inches. The length is measured from the point of the prosternum or breast bone to the rear edge of the pelvis, the ischial tuberosity.

BODY

The whole structure of the body gives an impression of depth and solidity without bulkiness. *Chest:* Commencing at the prosternum, it is well filled and carried well down between the legs. It is deep and capacious, never shallow, with ample room for the lungs and heart, carried well forward, with the prosternum showing ahead of the shoulder in profile. *Ribs:* Well sprung and long, neither barrel-shaped nor too flat, and carried down to a sternum which reaches to the elbows. Correct ribbing allows the elbows to move back freely when the dog is at a trot. Too round causes interference and throws the elbows out; too flat or short causes pinched elbows. Ribbing is carried well back so that the loin is relatively short. *Abdomen:* Firmly held and not paunchy. The bottom line is only moderately tucked up in the loin.

TOPLINE

Withers: The withers are higher than and sloping into the level back. *Back:* The back is straight, very strongly developed without sag or roach, and relatively short. The desirable long proportion is not derived from a long back, but from over-all length with relation to height, which is achieved by length of forequarter and length of withers and hindquarter, viewed from the side. *Loin:* Viewed from the top, broad and strong. Undue length between the last rib and the thigh, when viewed from the side, is undesirable. *Croup:* Long and gradually sloping.

TAIL

Bushy, with the last vertebra extended at least to the hock joint. It is set smoothly into the croup and low rather than high. At rest, the tail hangs in a slight curve like a saber. A slight hook—sometimes carried to one side—is faulty only to the extent that it mars general appearance. When the dog is excited or in motion, the curve is accentuated and the tail raised, but it should never be curled forward beyond a vertical line.

Tails too short, or with clumpy ends due to ankylosis, are serious faults. A dog with a docked tail must be disqualified.

HINDQUARTERS

The whole assembly of the thigh, viewed from the side, is broad, with both upper and lower thigh well muscled, forming as nearly as possible a right angle. The upper thigh bone parallels the shoulder blade while the lower thigh bone parallels the upper arm. The metatarsus (the unit between the hock joint and the foot) is short, strong and tightly articulated.

GAIT

A German Shepherd Dog is a trotting dog, and its structure has been developed to meet the requirements of its work. *General Impression:* The gait is outreaching, elastic, seemingly without effort, smooth and rhythmic covering the maximum amount of ground with the minimum number of steps. At a walk it covers a great deal of ground, with long stride of both hind legs and forelegs. At a trot the dog covers still more ground with even longer stride, and moves powerfully but

Excellent rear

Cowhocked, dewclaws

An excellent mover this dog shows reach in front, power behind, and transmission of hind thrust through his iron back.

easily, with co-ordination and balance so that the gait appears to be the steady motion of a well-lubricated machine. The feet travel close to the ground on both forward reach and backward push. In order to achieve ideal movement of this kind, there must be good muscular development and ligamentation. The hindquarters deliver, through the back, a powerful forward thrust which slightly lifts the whole animal and drives the body forward. Reaching far under, and passing the imprint left by the front foot, the hind foot takes hold of the ground; then hock, stifle and upper thigh come into play and sweep back, the stroke of the hind leg finishing with the foot still close to the ground in a smooth follow-through. The over-reach of the hindquarter usually necessitates one hind foot passing outside and the other hind foot passing inside the track of the forefeet, and such action is not faulty unless the locomotion is crabwise with the dog's body sideways out of the normal straight line.

TRANSMISSION

The typical smooth, flowing gait is maintained with great strength and firmness of back. The whole effort of the hindquarter is transmitted to the forequarter through the loin, back and withers. At full trot, the back must remain firm and level without sway, roll, whip or roach. Unlevel topline with withers lower than the hip is a fault. To compensate for the forward motion imparted by the hindquarters, the shoulder should open to its full extent. The forelegs should reach out close to the ground in a long stride in harmony with that of the hindquarters. The dog does not track on widely separated parallel lines, but brings the feet inward toward the middle line of the body when trotting in order to maintain balance. The feet track closely but do not strike or cross over. Viewed from the front, the front legs function from the shoulder joint to the pad in a straight line. Viewed from the rear, the hind legs function from the hip joint to the pad in a straight line. Faults of gait, whether from front, rear or side, are to be considered very serious faults.

Ch. Atlas v. Elfenhain, one of the famous "A" litter Elfenhain, sired by a great dog, Grimm v.d. Fahrmuhle. Atlas, now deceased, was imported to the U.S. by Rudy Reinker. Note the beautiful front and shoulder assembly of this animal, virtues so difficult to achieve and hold.

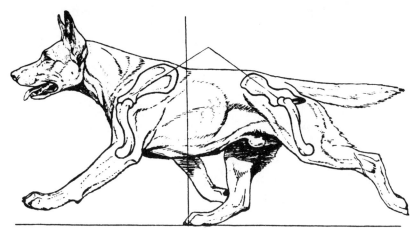

The balanced, extended trot specific to the German Shepherd dog.

COLOR
The German Shepherd Dog varies in color, and most colors are permissible. Strong, rich colors are preferred. Nose black. Pale, washed-out colors and blues or livers are serious faults. A white dog or a dog with a nose that is not predominantly black, must be disqualified.

COAT
The ideal dog has a double coat of medium length. The outer coat should be as dense as possible, hair straight, harsh and lying close to the body. A slightly wavy outer coat, often of wiry texture, is permissible. The head, including the inner ear and foreface, and the legs and paws are covered with short hair, and the neck with longer and thicker hair. The rear of the forelegs and hind legs has somewhat longer hair extending to the pastern and hock, respectively. Faults in coat include soft, silky, too long outer coat, woolly, curly, and open coat.

DISQUALIFICATIONS
Cropped or hanging ears. Undershot jaw. Docked tail. White dogs. Dogs with noses not predominantly black. Any dog that attempts to bite the judge.

A good young sable male with a very expressive head.

This, then, is the official standard of the German Shepherd Dog, issued by the German Shepherd Dog Club of America and approved by the American Kennel Club. If you read it diligently you will realize how different interpretations by various judges and breeders can bring varied meaning to many of the passages. Comparison is also a very real factor to be considered. For instance, what is a "relatively long" neck? The shoulder blades are "not placed forward"—from what? Incidentally, there are seven bones in the Shepherd's neck, the same as in all mammals, from the giraffe to the whale, and to man. And the shoulders of the Shepherd float free, held to the rest of the skeletal structure by ligaments and muscles. The dog does not possess a clavicle (or collarbone). Only mammals who reach above their heads with their front arms and feet need clavicles.

I would propose to the powers that be that a point scale be offered as a guide to arrive at a more accurate appraisal of the German Shepherd. Many standards do offer such a yardstick for measuring worth, but not the Shepherd standard. I suggest the following point scale for the German Shepherd Dog.

GENERAL CONFORMATION
AND APPEARANCE
    Proportions 6
    Bone and Substance 6
    Temperament 8
    Nobility 3
    Condition 3

HEAD
    Shape 4
    Teeth 4
    Eyes 2
    Ears 4

NECK
    Length, crest 2

BODY
    Withers, Backline,
        Loin, Croup 10
    Chest, Brisket, Ribs 8
    Shape and Proportions . . 3

FOREQUARTERS
    Shoulder 5
    Legs, Pasterns, Paws . . . 2
    Angulation 5

HINDQUARTERS
    Thigh, Stifle, Hocks 3
    Angulation 5
    Paws 2

GAIT
    Walk and Trot 10

COAT
    Color, Texture,
        Markings 5

TOTAL . . . . 100 points

This point system need not be accepted arbitrarily: it is certainly open to change with a point or points removed from one area and added to another. But it is a suggested base for a breed point scale that can bring a bit of mathematical precision to the standard.

BIBLIOGRAPHY

Arenas, N., and Sammartino, R., Le Cycle Sexuel de la Chienne. *Etude Histol.*
Bull. Histol. Appl. Physiol. et Path., 16:299, 1939.
Ash, E. C., *Dogs: Their History and Development*, 2 vols., London, 1927.
Barrows, W. M., *Science of Animal Life*. New York, World Book Co., 1927.
Burns, Marca, 1952. The Genetics of the Dog, Comm. Agri. Bur., Eng. 122 pp.
Castle, W. E., *Genetics and Eugenics*, 4th ed. Cambridge, Mass., Harvard
University Press, 1930.
Darwin, C., *The Variation of Animals and Plants Under Domestication*, New
York, D. Appleton Co., 1890.
Davenport, C. B., *Heredity in Relation to Eugenics*. New York, Henry Holt &
Co., Inc., 1911.
Hart, E. H., "Artificial Insemination." *Your Dog*, March, 1948.
——— "The Judging Situation." *Your Dog*, March, 1948.
——— Doggy Hints. *Men Mg*. Zenith Pub. Co., 1950.
——— "Judgment Day." *Shep. Dog Rev.*, Jan., 1953.
——— *This is the Puppy*, T.F.H. Publications, Inc., 1962.
——— *This is the Weimaraner*, T.F.H. Publications, Inc., 1965.
——— *Your Poodle Puppy*, T.F.H. Publications, Inc., 1966.
——— *The Poodle Handbook*, T.F.H. Publications, Inc., 1966.
——— *This is the Great Dane*, T.F.H. Publications, Inc., 1967.
——— *Dog Breeders' Handbook*, T.F.H. Publications, Inc., 1967.
——— *How to Train Your Dog*, T.F.H. Publications, Inc., 1967.
——— *Enclyopedia of Dog Breeds*, T.F.H. Publications, Inc., 1967.

Hermansson, K. A., "Artificial Impregnation of the Dog." *Svensk. Vet. Tidshr.*,
39:382, 1934.
Humphrey, E. S. "Mental Tests for Shepherd Dogs." *J. of Hered.*, 25:129, 1934.
——— , and Warner, Lucien, *Working Dogs*. Baltimore, Johns Hopkins Press,
1934.
Keeler, C. E., and Trimble, H. C., "Inheritance of Dewclaws." *J. of Hered.*,
29:145, 1938.
Krushinsky, L. A., "A Study of the Phenogenetics of Behaviour Characters in
Dogs." *Biol. Journ. T.*, VII, No. 4, Inst. Zool., Moscow State Univ., 1938.
MacDowell, E. C., "Heredity of Behaviour in Dogs," Dept. of Genetics,
Yearbook, Carn. Inst., No. 20, 101-56, 1921.
Muller, Friedrich, *Geschichte des Verein fur Deutsche Schaferhunde.* 1899-1949.
S.V., Augsburg, 1949.
Nagel, W. A., Der Farbensinn des Hundes. *Zbl. Physiol.*, 21, 1907.
Whitney, L. F., *The Basis of Breeding.* N. H. Fowler, 1928.
——— *How To Breed Dogs*. New York, Orange Judd Pub. Co., 1947.
——— *Feeding Our Dogs*. New York, D. van Nostrand Co. Inc., 1949.
——— *Complete Book of Dog Care*, Garden City, L.I., Doubleday & Co. Inc.,
1953.
——— and Whitney, G. D., *The Distemper Complex*. Orange, Conn., Practical
Science Pub. Co., 1953.

INDEX